Nebraska Presence: An Anthology of Poetry

DATE DUE

Nebraska

Presence

* * *

An Anthology of Poetry
Greg Kosmicki and Mary K. Stillwell, Editors

The Backwaters Press

First Printing: October, 2007

Cover art by Stephen Dinsmore, "Interior, the Studio," Copyright 2007 © Stephen Dinsmore, used by permission of the artist.

Cover design by Bristol Creative, www.bristolcreative.com
Book Design by The Backwaters Press
Special thanks to Sarah Voss, for assistance with text issues.

Published by   The Backwaters Press
                Greg Kosmicki, Rich Wyatt, Editors
                Mary K. Stillwell, Guest Editor for
                Nebraska Presence: An Anthology of Poetry
                3502 North 52nd Street
                Omaha, Nebraska 68104-3506

                (402) 451-4052
                www.thebackwaterspress.homestead.com
                gkosmicki@cox.net

ISBN: 0-9793934-3-4
13 digit ISBN: 978-0-9793934-3-3

Introduction: Whys and Wherefores

Poets and Their Works

"Artistic growth is, more than it is anything else, a refining of the sense of truthfulness. The stupid believe that to be truthful is easy; only the artist, the great artist, knows how difficult it is."

—Willa Cather in *Song of the Lark*

"This they tell, and whether it happened so or not, I do not know; but if you think about it, you can see that it is true."

—Black Elk, in *Black Elk Speaks*, as quoted by John G. Niehardt

"What I think poetry can do is give people fresh ways to look at the world."

—Ted Kooser

For Nebraskans, Far and Near

Whys and Wherefores...an Introduction

Greg Kosmicki

Why did you decide to publish an anthology of Nebraska poetry?

I had been thinking about it around the turn of the century, because it's a pretty big deal to get to the end of a century and the start of another one, not to mention a millennium. Most people reading this won't live to the end of the next century and even fewer of us will live till the next millennium, so it seemed like a propitious time. I thought it would be a fun thing to capture a snapshot of the poetry being written in Nebraska at the beginning of the new century. If nothing else, it will give the poets in 2099 something to look back upon and pause for a moment to see how their work has advanced. Who knows? By 2099, writing as we know it today, and poetry as we know it today, may be obsolete. Maybe people won't need it anymore. Maybe they won't need air anymore either—we'll see—or someone will.

I was sitting at my press' table at the Nebraska Book Festival in Kearney (will they still have books in 2099?) and a very good Nebraska poet this press has published twice, and who has edited two books published by this press, Marjorie Saiser, popped up at my table and said "You ought to do an anthology of Nebraska poetry!" She must have been reading my mind, because it was not long before, it seems like it was only a couple weeks, that a poet living just north of Lincoln, Ted Kooser, was named Poet Laureate of the United States, and I was sitting there thinking that I should do an anthology of Nebraska poets.

I told her that I would do the anthology if she would help edit, and she, having spent the better part of two years cleaning up my messes for an anthology of Great Plains/ High Plains writing by women, said, well, she said "No." But she said she'd think of someone who would be good for that job, and let me know.

The name she came up with is the name of a person who was to became my co-editor and my friend, Mary K. Stillwell. We met once, and then as life does, life intervened, and we were not able to meet again for nearly a year. We re-set our time lines, jiggled our compasses to get the dust out of them, and set off on our voyage to the inland sea of Nebraska poetry once again.

How did you get the word out to poets far and near on the anthology?

We got the word out to poets by word-of-mouth, advertisements in *Poets & Writers* Classifieds, personal letters to poets, and e-mails to poets we knew outside of the state.

What was the selection process like? How did it work?

We read for content and for the use of language, aural language as well as written. We read most if not all of the poems in the anthology out loud to each other, especially because we wanted to hear the poems that had been initially "published" in open-mike readings and then later collected in open-mike anthologies, to be certain that we were giving them a fair reading.

What did you look for in a poem for the anthology?

My personal criteria for any poem is that it does what Emily Dickinson says what a poem does—that it takes the top of your head off. Naturally, this is a messy process, and I spent a lot of time in the ER having my head fixed, but we got a good anthology out of it, so it was worth it.

Did Nebraska content take precedence?

No, we specifically stated in our letter requesting poets to send in poems that the poems did not have to have a Nebraska theme, though several poets did write back to us asking if the poems had to be Nebraska-themed or rural-themed. We told them, "No." But we still got a few poems about farm animals and barns.

What has been the biggest surprise you experienced in the process?

That we were actually able to get the materials together and keep them organized, since I am challenged in that area.

Would you change eligibility requirements if you were to do it over again?

We were aiming to get an anthology of high literary quality that would be able to be compared favorably with any other anthology from any part of the country. Our aim was not to get a cross-section of all the writers in Nebraska who have ever written a poem but who may not really think of themselves as poets, or as their calling as being poets. We were looking for poets who have taken it seriously enough that they have spent a considerable amount of time with it in trying to get their poems printed in literary magazines and periodicals, and whose poems were of a high enough level of literary quality that they were able to get them published in magazines that are run by people they don't know, or in magazines other than student or writing-group magazines, or in magazines whose editors aren't familiar with their writing already. But there are many poets in the state who are working at their poetry who aren't quite at that level, who I would like to include, to get more of cross section of all the poetry that's going on in the state. So, maybe the press will do another anthology in a few years with less stringent threshold submission requirements. We relaxed the literary publication requirements to some degree because we hoped to find written-out work by performance or slam poets that worked well on the page, but not the requirement for residency.

Are you planning an anthology of poets who may have lived and/or studied here but have moved on?

We have talked about that, and I am thinking about it. There are many excellent poets who moved away who spent most of their early lives or their formative years here but who may not have been born here, or who went to a college or university here and stayed around a while and then moved on. So, it would be an interesting anthology. Perhaps unwieldy. Another idea I've been tossing around is an anthology of poems about Nebraska by just anybody who may have driven through the state by accident, say, to get to Colorado, or who re-routed their trip to Montana just to go see Carhenge north of Alliance, or Fort Robinson west of Crawford, where Crazy Horse was murdered. There may be an entire cottage industry waiting to blossom around Nebraska and poetry. Who knows?

Was it difficult to choose or not choose poems from poets you knew well or had already published?

Sometimes my favorite poems that we received from poets that I have published in book form previously were not the favorites of my co-editor, and sometimes the poets didn't send the ones that were my favorites to us to consider. But I liked all the poems the poets wrote anyway, or the large majority of them, or I wouldn't have published their books in the first place, so I picked from among the poems the poet sent, rather than to contact them to ask for one of my personal favorites. I think that it's good to get the attention onto other poems anyway, rather than just the "signature" poems, because all poets who have worked at writing to the point that they have had at least one collection published have many many poems they have written that deserve attention. A collection is literally only the tip of the iceberg, as any poet can tell you. Or maybe more like a crystal of ice on the tip of the tip of the iceberg.

Any surprises among the poems you received?

At the risk of sounding like a smart-aleck (whatever that means) all the poems have surprises in them, or they would not be good poems. So, the answer is yes.

Why do you think Nebraska currently has such a vibrant reading and writing community?

I think that it is the result of many years of nurturing by many fine poets, both in academia and outside of it. We have had, and have, some world-class teachers of poetry and the art of writing poetry, and the art of being a poet here in our state. I don't want to name names for fear of leaving someone out, but the poets who have been here teaching for 30 or 40 years have taught a myriad of poets how to be poets, who have taught others. Because of them, we have literary presses, we have nationally-acclaimed literary magazines and several others across the state that attract submissions from all over the country. We have poets who have trained here and gone on to teach at prestigious universities, win prizes, and edit well-known magazines. We have a poet living here who is a Pulitzer Prize Winner and former Poet Laureate. We have writing groups everywhere—hundreds of them. We have reading groups. We have nationally-known scholars. We have nationally-known cowboy poets. We have national contender poetry slam teams. We've got open mikes and slams and readings all over the place, and more of them popping up like dandelions after a spring rain. We've got websites devoted to Nebraska writers. We've got e-mail listings of poetry events. We've got a state-supported Poets-in-the-Schools program. We've got a State Poet. One of our universities even erected a statue in honor of (gasp!) a living poet.

Any hunches for the future à la Carnac the Magnificent of what the future of NE poetry might hold?

Nobody knows the future, except Carnac, and we all know what happened to him. I think that it will continue to grow in Nebraska, and everywhere, as more and more people will continue seek the answer to the mysteries of life in poetry. Many of us are familiar with the famous William Carlos Williams (not a Nebraskan) quote about poetry:

> Look at
> > what passes for the new.
> > > You will not find it there but in
>
> despised poems.
> > It is difficult
> > > to get the news from poems
>
> yet men die miserably every day
> > for lack
> > > of what is found there.

Poets from Nebraska well know what is found in their despised poems, and the differences that they can make.

Mary K. Stillwell

How did you come to co-edit Nebraska Presence?

I received an email from a *gkosmicki* several years ago and, despite the subject line—"Opportunity to Work Your Socks Off for No Pay"—like Pandora, I just couldn't leave well enough alone. The rest, as they say, is history.

Even without socks, however, I'm grateful for having had the opportunity to work with Greg in bringing together some of the best Nebraska poetry of our time. We received almost one-hundred and fifty submissions, over fifteen hundred pages of poetry, from all over the state and from as far away as Sweden. The quality of the work was nearly uniformly high which made the final selection very difficult.

Why did you and do you think an anthology is a worthwhile venture, given all the work it involves?

Walt Whitman said, "To have great poets there must be great audiences," and we are fortunate here in Nebraska that so many people read poetry, as well as go to poetry readings. Each semester when I ask students to bring in their favorite poems, they bring in Mother Goose, Dr. Seuss, and Edward Lear, and they also bring in poems by William Blake, Emily Dickenson, Bashō, Edgar Allen Poe (a big favorite), and a sampling of Nebraska poets. Their teachers and the poets who visit their classrooms in primary and secondary schools are doing a fine job introducing a variety of poets and poetic traditions. Some students take part in recitations at speech meets around the state; for the last two years, a young Nebraskan has represented our state at the Poetry Out Loud National Recitation Contest in Washington, D. C. A number of my students, by the time they have arrived at college, have already *written* poetry. I think an anthology can and will stimulate the reading and writing of poetry even more.

Why do you think so many Nebraskans read and write poetry?

Poetry has been a way of life for residents here for as far back as we can trace. James R. Murie's account of the rituals of the Skidi band of the Pawnee in *Ceremonies of the Pawnee*, for example, gives us at least a small taste of the poetry and song of early residents who hunted across the native prairies and farmed the land along the streams.

White settlers brought another kind of poetry with them. The inaugural issue of the *Nebraska Palladium*, the first newspaper published in the Nebraska Territory, carried the poem "A Lady Type Setter" by T. D. Curtis on July 15, 1854, according to Bernice Slote's research notes. Joseph Wydevan reports that the first anthology of 32 Nebraska poets, *Nebraska Poets: One Hundred Pages of Prairie Poems,* was published in 1893. Early newspapers record the meetings of literary societies and library clubs in river towns—Omaha, Nebraska City, Brownville, Falls City—as these areas were settled by the new wave of men and women arriving after the end of the Civil War. As white settlement spread across the Territory, so did the "literaries." Newcomers brought their favorite poems and songs in books and memory. According to Mel Krutz's *Reading and Writing Nebraska: A Survey of Our State's Book Discussion and Writing Groups,* eight Nebraska book clubs that began in the 1890s are still meeting today.

Germans, Scandinavians, French, Bohemians, and other immigrant groups brought their literature with them as they made their homes here. I remember my stepfather's father reciting poems in German and French after dinner on Sundays. I knew him as a retired farmer in Richardson County, but long before his farming days, he was a literature student in Germany. Alvin Johnson, born on a farm outside Homer in 1874, wrote about the influence of a neighbor, Professor Winkhaus, a German philosopher who had turned to farming in Nebraska. Johnson, who grew up to edit the *New Republic* and serve as a director of the New School for Social Research, heard about Hegel, Schopenhauer, and Kant, as well as German poets and writers, whenever he visited the Winkhaus farm. Some neighbors thought Winkhaus "brain-broke," however, because of his interest in things other than farming. Willa Cather, of course, has given us several fictional examples of immigrant artists for whom farming proves fatal: Peter from an early short story of the same name and Mr. Shimerda in *My Ántonia* are two who come to mind.

Contemporary Nebraska writers also have many examples of fine writers who have gone before us. There's Willa Cather, of course, as well as Wright Morris, Weldon Kees, Mari Sandoz, Loren Eiseley, and others. John Neihardt is probably the best known poet from the early part of the twentieth century, primarily for *Black Elk Speaks: Being the Life Story of a Holy Man of the Oglala Sioux* published in 1932. Beatrice native, Weldon Kees, has become a late 20th century cult icon.

Or, it could be, as I've suspected all along, there's something in the Ogallala aquifer that has promoted poetry all across the plains.

Is there a relationship between Nebraska poetry and American poetry in general?

Very much so. Nebraska poets have been supported and informed by one of the oldest literary journals in the United States, *Prairie Schooner.* Founded in 1926 by Lowry C. Wimberly, *PS* published poets from the plains alongside poets from other parts of the US—and beyond, establishing a kind of conversation that went well beyond state or regional or even national boundaries. Karl Shapiro, who had a tremendous influence on Nebraska poetry, took over the editorship of *Prairie Schooner* in 1956. Shapiro, former U.S. Poet Laureate (or Consultant in Poetry to the Library of Congress, as the position was called then), Pulitzer Prize winner, and editor of *Poetry* magazine, was vehemently opposed (and even this may be an understatement) to the elitism he saw in T. S. Eliot and Ezra Pound and the pedantry of New Criticism.

According to Shapiro, Eliot and Pound—along with I. A. Richards, James Joyce, W. B. Yeats, and Wallace Stevens—wrote "diseased art." Instead, Shapiro looked to Robert Frost, Isabella Gardner, and William Carlos Williams for "real" American poetry, which he published in *PS* and taught at the University. Like Williams ("no ideas but in things"), Shapiro advocated going to the world directly rather than via abstraction; the use of the American idiom, the variable foot, and the natural line break, which is close to the rule in *Nebraska Presence.* Don Jones' use of Williams' stepped triadic lines is a testimony to his influence. Jones, Kloefkorn, Kooser, Scheele, and Welch—and likely others between the covers of this anthology—were students of Shapiro. Jones' and Kooser's first books were published through Shapiro's advocacy.

Would you say more about the influence of Karl Shapiro?

Shapiro's interest in prosody was profound, and he made certain his students were well grounded in it. Don Welch writes that Shapiro "would occasionally bring a poem submitted to the *Schooner* for us to analyze. I remember one poem was from Auden, and about gout. Talk about intimidating. Shapiro not only wanted to know what its rhythm was, and how it fit in historically, but if it were good enough to publish." Kloefkorn's experience was similar. He recalls Shapiro's "enormous respect for words."

Shapiro—along with then-doctoral student Robert Beum, who taught at Creighton University—wrote *A Prosody Handbook* while he taught in Nebraska. The handbook was reissued by Dover just last year, a testimony to its excellence. Shapiro's students were also his legacy to the state; Kloefkorn, Kooser, Scheele, Welch, and others remained here to write, read, and teach, influencing subsequent generations of poets.

Is there such a thing as Nebraska poetry then?

This is a question I'm asked with some frequency, along with its companion,—"If so, what makes our poems different from the poems written by poets in or from other states and other places?"

As I read through the final manuscript of *Nebraska Presence,* I thought a good deal about these questions and also recalled Thomas McGrath's statement that he didn't think regional values were particularly unique, only what he termed as "variants of national values." That's probably true of the *Nebraska Presence* poems.

Or perhaps the question is no longer relevant. Nebraska's native prairie is mostly gone, the rivers have been diverted, the birds and other wildlife diminished, the earth divided into right-angled sections. We've "humanized" our place so profoundly that old assumptions are called to question:: Does the *horizon* itself still speak here? Does *distance* speak? *New York Quarterly* editor Bill Packard used to say that regional poetry was being replaced by what he called a "bevy of special interests;" we think in terms of feminist, Native, Chicago, academic, gay, cowboy, and/or white-guy poetry.

Still, it does seem that the language of our place is reflected in our vocabulary, our colloquialisms, our speech patterns, and our syntax, and these give our poems a particular sensibility and resonance. Just how that occurs is something I'll be puzzling over for some time to come. This is something I'd like to hear back from other readers and writers about too.

Surely we see themes repeating thoughout the anthology. Loss is one of them: death of parents and grandparents, ex-husbands, of birds, of faith; the passage of time, loss of innocence, the potential end of the human race! Poems address the events of September 11th, the war in Iraq, Homeland Security, and the continuing depletion of our natural resources. Twyla Hansen, for example, tells about hearing the news of the collapse of the twin towers while walking with children on Nine-mile Prairie. On the one hand we ask, as Hansen does, "How do we comprehend fanatics?" and on the other, we are reminded by the poem that on this prairie "blameless" Native children died, that the fanatics, at times, have been us.

History, plains and world, is a integral to many of these poems that address loss in some way: Sweatshop piece-work in Grace Bauer's "Modern Clothing," child abuse, teen pregnancy, how the "wayward girls of Omaha, Nebraska, 1965" fared at "Booth Charity Hospital bare / as cloister cells" in Susan Aizenberg's "Debut: Late Lines for a Thirtieth Birthday," as well as in the poems mentioned above. Ron Block gives us a poem set off in quotes. We have to pay attention to the story, get involved with what's going on in order to make sense of it, and by its conclusion, he has us wondering about the Nebraska that's "a dark passage that no one wants / to make awake." This is a poem about a Nebraska shadow with its heightening of sexuality and erasure of the flesh and blood woman (among other things), about our level of consciousness and denial.

We have a considerable amount of shadow collected here, which isn't really surprising since art is, in general, subversive by digging below the surface of the cliché. Poetry frequently asks us to look at our lives, habits, mortality, and our places in ways that sometimes make us uncomfortable. Poetry can provide the grist—"radiant grist" as William Carlos Williams would say—from which transformation, in consciousness and even in revolution, can arise. After all, poetry is, as Greg Kuzma says in *What Poetry is All About,* "the purest form of self adventure."

Is this unique to Nebraska poetry?

Poetry can help, Kuzma continues, "remedy this awful business of our living. Oh words in a beautiful order, come soon into my ears and tongue, so that I may not feel so utterly doomed and alone." Nebraskans are not alone in the universe, and our concerns are the concerns of those across the country and around the world. Perhaps Pandora would see one aspect of poetry as a sign of hope. Judging by this anthology, poetry mirrors and directs our attention to the importance of joy, solace, tenderness, and connectedness in the making of meaning, even in a time of loss.

Interconnectedness—geographically, temporally, and through relationship with others—begins with the first poem in the book, "On the Pleasant Valley Road," by Lucy Adkins. The form of the poem, which is one sentence long, reinforces that connection; there is only one road that connects all of us who live under the shine of "God's stars." The title serves as the poem's first line that the reader follows beside those familiar farmhouses with armed service stars (blue for service and "gold for the dead") in the windows between Palmer and Fullerton and on to bomber plants (recalling for Nebraskans that the Enola Gay, the B-29 that dropped the world's first atomic bomb, was built in Omaha). The road goes on to connect us to shipyards of the Nation's coasts, to the death camps at Auschwitz and Dachau and on to Hiroshima where the bomb killed tens of thousands more. Historical connection is ironically underscored in Mordecai Marcus' "Always Back There" and again in Ernst Niemann's "Refusal to Apologize for the Way Things Are."

Bill Kloefkorn's "Connections: A Toast" and "My Love for All things Warm and Breathing," both one (long) sentence poems, celebrate relationship with human beings, from Aeschylus to Rosa Parks, Bach to Pee Wee Reese, and to all things—the bur oak, hot dogs, saddle and horse—that make up "one / steady and diverse and universal song." We seem to have a great belief in absence and distance, but it is not just the absence of the past that informs Nebraska poetry; it is also the absence of the future, vibrant with possibilities.

Perhaps that's why I opened that e-mail. Connection gives us, among other things, *hope,* and an anthology of contemporary Nebraska poetry offers us both connection and conversation. When I was a kid living in southeast Nebraska, there was a café in town called the "Chat and Nibble," where all the farmers, their families, and town folks, gathered every Saturday afternoon to rub shoulders, swap stories, and catch up on the news over a glass of beer or cup of coffee. Our sense of community was enhanced through the sharing of hopes and dreams—as well as useful information. Years later, as an adult and living elsewhere, my visits home always included a trip to the café to see what was happening, to listen to the local melody that weaves into what Kloefkorn describes as that "one / steady and diverse and universal song."

What *Nebraska Presence* provides, like my hometown's café on Stone Street, is an intergenerational meeting place for readers and poets—for whom writing is a solitary art—to gather side by side and talk. There is a real pleasure in knowing such a community exists and in belonging to it; it allows us to swap stories and ideas, find out what everyone's been doing, and maybe even catch a glimpse of what the future might hold.

Nebraska Presence: An Anthology of Poetry

Lucy Adkins

On the Pleasant Valley Road
(Nance County 1941-45)

that rolls from Palmer to Fullerton
all the farmhouses sit square
to the road, and there are stars in the windows
for those at war:
    blue stars for service
    gold for the dead
and above, all God's stars shining,
their light weak and cold
but shining
over these little farms,
over the farmers and farmwives,
the much-beloved sons,
the skinny-armed daughters;
and in cities and towns
shining over the bomber plants,
over schoolyards and shipyards,
shining down, too, over France and Italy,
over the darkness of Poland and Romania,
over Auschwitz and Dachau, the furnaces
stoked and blazing,
and Hiroshima where all the lights
went out.

Susan Aizenberg

Debut: Late Lines for a Thirtieth Birthday

> *Adoptees do not have the luxury of envisioning their celebrated births...they*
> *often know nothing of their debuts...*
>   Jan L. Waldron, *Giving Away Simone*

You say you can't sleep nights, imagining them,
  the wayward girls of Omaha, Nebraska, 1965,
the chill green rooms of Booth Charity Hospital bare
  as cloister cells, where they'll labor hard—*learn*

their lesson, the doctor says—and leave the infants
  they may name but not hold. It's the weekly outing
that gets you. Movies the Junior League springs for,
  something sweet at Dairy Queen, how, docile

as calves, they're led in line by twos, a few holding
  hands like the schoolgirls they are. But look—here's
your mother, the copper hair she'll pass to you
  mirroring the late September sun, that same glamour-

puss mole etched on the still soft curve of her cheek.
  She won't line up, doesn't want ice cream, waits
outside, slouched against a red Mustang she'd like
  to own, smoking the Old Golds she knows say

bad girl, even now. Along the empty street,
  this part of town where no one comes, the first leaves
drop to skitter along the gutter, make her think
  of snow, of the movie they've just seen—Lean's

Zhivago and Lara warm with vodka and lovemaking
  in a glistening blizzard of a house, snow veiling everything,
the gas lamps and satin couches, even the poet's desk
  slick with frost, of their lost daughter, how years

later, she refuses the proffered gift of her past.
  No Slavic romance in your mother's past,
just some west Nebraska town so small it's no more
  than a stutter in the long silence of the prairie,

her father's strap, regular as church once she began
  to show, the pursed mouth of her mother, a Greyhound
into this dirty city, where for days she slept and read
  from a book of names, choosing *Helen* for you,

maybe thinking of those thousand ships, maybe
  of some favorite teacher, one who called her writing
good. You can't know any of this, anymore than she knows
  it's just hours from your birth. I like to think you'll arrive

through a shared dream of iced and glittering Russian
  trees, Yuri smiling at the first sun he's seen in months
before turning to his work, that you debut to a welcoming
  chorus of *troika* bells and *balalaikas*, a cry of wolves.

Things That Cannot Be Compared (Dissonance I)

after Sei Shonagon

My father's hand, elegant as typescript, before his stroke. My mother's lefty scrawl, the way she underlined _We_ on my birthday card—_We wish you much happiness!_—four months after his death. The deep green of this morning's lowering cloudbank, sea lettuce riding the Intertidal. Bleached sheet of the sky back home, Nebraska heat shimmering above the stunned soy fields. Miraculous snowy egret, tall as a woman, feeding with genteel *sang-froid* on palm fronds outside my mother's kitchen window, so close we might have touched her swanny neck. Black bear cub, lost last night in the widening dark glade beyond the yellow hoops of porch lights, who would not be lured to safety by the game warden's stale doughnuts Shrill song of gulls scavenging. The flutter and purr of Carolina locusts.

When one has stopped loving someone, one feels that person has become someone else, even though he is the same person.

Substitute *ghost. A question of mourning. Unable to mourn.*

Red hour of the wolf. No sound except the whirr of fan blades above our borrowed bed, the silvery notes of my mother's wooden cuckoo. She believes it herald of my father's spirit. Each hour I hear it crow, bright cry rising from its mechanical throat like the freed breath of sleepers. It wakes me from my dream of her overlit kitchen, the negative space before the window where my father is not standing, transfixed by the egret, calling to me to *Come, see!* Where he does not wince as I join him, recoil from his kiss.

DENISE BANKER

Bed Fellows

Each night is ritual.
The florist's five-year-old daughter
Counts the brush strokes
The old woman seated at the vanity
Pulls through her long white hair.
And Death is there.

She is in bed with them, too.
The three of them, tucked under a shroud
Of pressed, bleached-white cotton.

Death dwells in the old woman's liver
Shrivels the organ with her sour, pasty breath.
And, even though the old woman and child sleep,
Death never rests, until her job is done.

How close Death is to the child.
How Death is the old woman, warming her feet
Against the child's; turning in the blankets
To face her, to kiss her cheek, her forehead.
How the old woman is Death.

Now, the old woman gone and no one at home,
The florist-girl becomes a showroom ornament
Arranged between mum and azalea, cyclamen
And Persian violet.

A showy, nodding flower, she takes naps
In a coffin-sized cardboard box
On which she has glued gauze and ribbons,
Leaves and petals.

The box fits in the corner near the hollow
Tin heating-stove which, to bring on sleep,
She lightly kicks in a careless rhythm.
How cold it is without the others.

CAROLE BARNES-MONTGOMERY

Any Particular Joy

Dolly never married Tom
she meant to but
there were too many miles between them—
when her son was born she named him Tom.
she meant to marry the man who fathered him
but again...
too many miles
and there was the old dad to contend with
him and his ill humor and his bent mind
his cattle, land, horses
feeding sleds in winter
hayracks in summer
and the endless waving grasses
carpeting the distance
the milk pails
washtubs
prairie fires
they kept a woman busy so that when her hair thinned and
the old man died and young Tom went away to Chicago
she counted the years on her fingers
and came up with none
she remembered with
any
particular
joy

GRACE BAUER

Modern Clothing

Bent over Singers like saints
before altars, half the women
I knew sat, row after row, stitching
the pockets, inseams, cuffs and flies
of men's dress trousers and boys'
sports slacks. For forty hours a week
at *Modern Clothing* they labored themselves
into eyestrain and bad backs.
Now and then, one of them—
rushed into carelessness—would sew
through her own skin, the relentless machine
piercing three or four times
before her foot winced off the pedal
and the needle, stippled red, came to rest
against her finger bone, drab threads
imbedded in her flesh like a crude tattoo.

Piece Work, they called it. And for years
I saw my future there, hunched like my grandmother,
who worked waistbands and hauled home
bags of fabric scraps she stacked
in closets and corners. Having forgotten
what she was saving for, she continued,
for decades, to save until the room
we were forced to share left little room
for us, and I developed a need
for space, the urge to discard.

I despised every square inch of cloth
she found a use for: the mismatched
slip-covers and pillow cases, doll clothes
of severe navy serge, the piecemeal wardrobe
she persisted in wearing despite
drawers full of better dresses
she was saving *for good*—an occasion
I realized early on would never be
good enough for her to squander
on something store-bought, not made by her hands.
She died with her hoard still piling up—
a stash of stuff we deemed useless,
carted off to Goodwill, where today I am
searching for a bargain, hoping to find

something *vintage* perhaps, a garment
that has survived long enough to come back
into fashion, a remnant from a stranger's life
I can salvage and put to good use.

On Finding a Footnote To "Truckin'"

To roll along in an easy, untroubled way.
That's how the fine print defines
the word, and this, my friends,
is the Norton Anthology,
so we know it must be true.

They're explaining Diane Wakoski's line,
keep on truckin, to a world that's gone
three decades beyond the use of such lingo,
the hip talk of my youth grown archaic
while I was too busy struggling to get something said
to notice it getting gone.

I am, after all, of that generation
that *trucked* through the sixties. One of those
boomers who elevated *freak* into a compliment
and turned *party* into a verb. But now
we're long past the age we once thought we could never
trust anyone else beyond, and the X'ers
who have taken our place are pierced, tattooed
and dyed in ways we *freaks* would not have dreamed.

Wakoski's no longer the gun-toting moll
she posed as when I first fell in love
with words. Garcia's joined the *really* dead,
left his assets in litigation between two women
in suits and pearls. Even Mr. Natural has probably revised
his image via hairweaves and liposuction, and most nights
I'm too tired to party past ten.

We might have once called this turn of events
a *bummer*—a word the Norton, to my knowledge,
has yet to pin down for posterity, but meant,
if memory serves me right, the opposite of something
far out or *out of sight.* Oh, those shape shifters
of language: slang. Ibid. Ibid. Op cit.

And what a long strange trip it's been.

Stephen Behrendt

Hawk Shadow, Early May

This apparition now, midday—
this terrible shadow, dark, flat,
with extended wings, tail fanning behind,
that slides across the fieldgrass,
the spurge and emerging brome, alfalfa.
There, among the grasses, small ears angle inward,
whiskers twitch near eyes that dare not blink,
bodies crouch as the shadow passes them:
do they cool for just an instant,
as the sun is blocked, the warmth interrupted?

I look up, gauging from the sun's angle
where the red-tail must be.
My questions are less urgent,
uninvolved with life or death,
concealment, vulnerability,
careless move beneath dew-bent grasses,
sound or shuffle, shift of shadow.
Yearling or seasoned,
what does the fledging tell me, what betray
of prowess, acuity, or plain blind luck?

Here around me the warm silence rests;
windless, the pasture pauses, freeze-frame,
as the shadow slopes down eastward,
following the fall of field that way,
inscribes a lazy ellipse above the stream,
and is pierced without warning
by the hawk arrowing down, talons fore,
that parts the winter-wheat stubble, then rises,
the small tawny life suspended from those yellow hooks
dwindling, emptying into the bitter, blinding sky.

The November Hawk

For weeks it hung around, lurking on the fence
three feet from the feeders:
young hawk hunching without threat
while cardinals and finches prodded tubular feeders,
sifting millet from niger seed, thistle.
Day after day it appeared, watching them
with beak-sharp eyes, head cocking left, right.
At Thanksgiving, with company around the table,
we watched and wondered at a young red-tail
haunting the feeders, silent, curious.

Then, for days, no hawk, nor sign of him,
no vanilla-cream breast feathers ruffling in the wind,
as the last pods rattled from the locusts,
the squirrels hurried from the stubble fields
the last-gleaned cobs of feeder corn.

From the northwest, swooping down from Alberta,
rushed a bitter wind that shook the windows,
tore loose shingles and downspout,
then glazed them with a freezing rain.

Next morning, I picked up shingles and downspout
from the corner that shed them by the big old blue spruce.
Beneath the tree, in the lee of the trunk, lay the hawk.
Fallen on his back, he showed that same creamy breast
and what we had never seen:
the protruding ribs and wing-bones of bald starvation,
the terrible accusation of our unknowing indifference
to his orphaning, his foodless autumn,
who never learned to hunt his meat
but only watched the sated seed-eaters,
uncomprehending, helpless, dying day by day
from inside his magnificent, hollowing frame.

Brian Bengtson

A Cigarette with Loni

It is Thursday night,
ten days until rent is due;
her brittle-thin legs shake
as the wind skims past her,
like headlights on the pavement.

There is a desert in her eyes.
She pulls at the purple dress
Momma sent her with the money
to stay away from home.
Her hands quiver like a child.

She walks like a puppet
with three strings cut;
her ashen skin glows
under the streetlights
as she looks for a new man.

There is a struggle in her breath.
She clutches a wrinkled brown bag
and the malt liquor inside
with the same callused need
that held her pipe thirty minutes ago.

No familiar cars pass us
and she asks for a cigarette
like she is passing the basket
at a Sunday morning service.
We silently smoke and wait.

Ron Block

Strip Joint

"...I once took him to the train station
in Holdrege, seventy miles away from our home,
and the trains only go through Nebraska at night,
the middle of the night, cause they plan it that way,
cause I suppose Nebraska's a dark passage no one wants
to make awake and so I went with him and we got
there an hour early so no way would any dark train be
sneaking in without our knowing, nothing was gonna
come out of nowhere without our knowing,

so we went to find some place to eat
and the only place open was a bar so we
were just about to devour our hamburgers,
when she came on stage, a woman, probably the
only woman in Holdrege, and she started
dancing for the twenty, maybe thirty men who were
still up and about in Holdrege at that time of night—

Well my son and me, we chewed our hamburgers
and I couldn't help but duck a bit when her top
came off and I tried not to look at my son but I
couldn't look at her either so I stared at my hamburger
until I noticed no one else was looking at the woman cause
they were staring at a TV set above the bar,
a black and white one too, strange in itself,
until I saw it was the bar's surveillance camera
pointed at the stage but even so
I couldn't figure out why they were staring at the TV
instead of her. Maybe everyone was trying to be polite,
or maybe everybody's seen a naked dancing woman
in the flesh but nobody had really seen one
dancing naked on a black and white screen,
or maybe when a TV's on you can't help watching it,
and who knows what the woman thought of all this.
She just danced, and we just ate, and after
a time it didn't even seem like she was there...."

Shame

No room for her books in the new house in town,
and so her father, a farmer and a reader himself,
casts his almanac and railroad books into the pit
he's dug seven paces from the repossessed house,
and he holds her hand to show that such a loss
will not be hers alone. He wants to assure her:
his words go with hers, under the earth.

So what goes into her silence first is *The Curly Tops
at Cherry Farm*, then the child's book of phonemes
where the vowels shaped like monkeys work out the rules:
when two vowels go walking, the first one does the talking.
They fall face open at the bottom of the hole,
and she is very careful what she says after that
because neighbors will talk.

But she memorizes how the shadow of a cottonwood
gestures vaguely toward the pit. She marks
the hash marks of a broken fence. She draws a map
in a diary guarded by a latch and key where she
records her wishes when her mind is full
of what she can't have, so she can go back,
so maybe her father will have second thoughts like this—

when you read a wish and remember it again.
Maybe if she doesn't say a word, he'd take his back
as if he'd repossessed them by himself.
Or maybe her stories will come back on their own
to light and eyes, their wind: they'll fly
on ruffled pages back to her. Because there
are holes in the stories I would tell about her,

she tells me where to dig if I might wish to see
how pages fare for sixty years beneath the dirt. . . .
But are the stories still there? Or are they buried where
I wasn't listening? I feel ashamed.
Her stories are rare and carefully worded—
and I'm afraid of how much room there will be
in the house without her.

John Brehm

Sea of Faith

Once when I was teaching "Dover Beach"
to a class of freshmen, a young woman
raised her hand and said "I'm confused
about this 'Sea of Faith.'" "Well," I said,
"let's talk about it. We probably need
to talk a bit about figurative language.
What confuses you about it?"
"I mean, is it a real sea?" she asked.
"You mean, is it a real body of water
that you could point to on a map
or visit on a vacation?"
"Yes," she said. "Is it a *real* sea?"
Oh Christ, I thought, is this where we are?
Next year I'll be teaching them the alphabet
and how to sound words out.
I'll have to teach them geography, apparently,
before we can move on to poetry.
I'll have to teach them history, too—
a few weeks on the Dark Ages might be instructive.
"Yes," I wanted to say, "it is.
It is a real sea. In fact it flows
right into the Sea of Ignorance
IN WHICH YOU ARE DROWNING.
Let me throw you a Rope of Salvation
before the Sharks of Desire gobble you up.
Let me hoist you back up onto this Ship of Fools
so that we might continue our search
for the Fountain of Youth. Here, take a drink
of this. It's fresh from the River of Forgetfulness."
But of course I didn't say any of that.
I tried to explain in such a way
as to protect her from humiliation,
tried to explain that poets
often speak of things that don't exist.
It was only much later that I wished
I could have answered differently,
only after I'd betrayed myself
and been betrayed that I wished
it was true, wished there really was a Sea of Faith
that you could wade out into,
dive under its blue and magic waters,
hold your breath, swim like a fish
down to the bottom, and then emerge again

able to believe in everything, faithful
and unafraid to ask even the simplest of questions,
happy to have them simply answered.

Valid Photo Identification Required

I don't understand myself, nor do I know myself, nor
can I explain or prove who I am to anyone else.
All I know is that I'm a man who let his out-
of-state Driver's License expire and who
does not have his original Social Security Card,
(issued at birth?) or a copy of said document,
to obtain which one must have an unexpired
Diver's License, which requires, of course, a valid
Social Security Card. I needed something to get me
on a plane at LaGuardia. I did have a Birth Certificate,
and when I slid it tentatively under the bullet-proof
Plexiglas window at the Brooklyn Social Security Office
and said "What about this?" to the unexpectedly
sympathetic and ontologically sophisticated young
Asian-American man scanning my application
for a replacement card, he looked at me and said:
"This doesn't help. This just proves you were born.
We need proof of your *continued* existence."
I threw up my hands and looked down at my body,
as if to say, "Well, I'm standing here, aren't I?
I admit I have not done much with this life.
I have failed at love, let down my friends,
ignored my best instincts and given my worst ones
free play, but for better or worse I *have* continued
to exist. Because if I *hadn't* continued to exist
I wouldn't be contemplating all the joys and deep
satisfactions of non-existence, as I am right now.
I don't imagine the dead are required to show papers
at every river crossing, or that only those with valid
photo ID are allowed into the caldron, or the
harpsichord concert, as the case may be. Often I wake
at 3 a.m.," I wanted to tell him, "with the night terrors,
scrambled fears of death, which would be one
of the privileges conferred exclusively upon the living,
and often I wish I could forget myself completely,
forget the fragile, worried, rabbit-hearted self
that seems to run my life, forget the whole
nightmarish mess—I wouldn't have *that*

feeling if I hadn't continued to exist, would I?
It's true," I wanted to confess, "I have no children
to mirror me into the future, and mostly I only
half-inhabit the poems I've written, a ghostly
uneasy absence floating just below the lines.
In fact, from the Buddhist perspective
I don't exist, but neither do you, nor any of this.
A luminous emptiness is all there is."
Instead I tell him I just want to visit my parents,
for Christmas, in Nebraska, for christsakes.
Which was no help.

Robert Brooke

The Night My Father Killed My Dog

In the restaurant, white napkins and baroque
violins, while, over an appetizer of garlic
artichoke bruschetta, my father lists

the things he's slain: that rattlesnake
in the desert outside Taos, a host of
rainbow trout, that grey ground squirrel

that burrowed out under his sprinkler
system, just below the Bird of Paradise.
Since he retired, he's moved to Arizona

and the severing of certain ties to home
must be on his mind. As for me, I'm
thirty-five when this happens. I call

myself adult and am trying to relearn
how parents can be just people too. Especially
my parents, remarried now these twenty

years, both of them happier (I must confess)
than when brother and sister and I tried
so very hard to make them Family, or

make them want to be. So when Dad says
"in my whole life the hardest was when
I had to put Eiger down—Robert, do you

remember the German Shepherd we had
on Lake Street? I couldn't even tell your
mother when I took him to the vet. But

you kept fighting with the neighbor kids
and Eiger would fight too." And of course
I do remember—that black-and-tan shape

circling the back yard between the fence
and the day lilies, how warm his belly,
the smell of wet dog and dirt when I rested

on him in the living room. For a moment,
I am all of five again, and small, and
what I most want in all the world is some

protection against such smallness. But
the waiter brings chicken in dill and cream
and raspberry sauce and in that lull

I can't forgive him, can't forgive
the offhand lie of Eiger running
on a farm outside Evergreen, and I

can't forgive myself for believing
it for almost thirty years. But he's
already forgotten and my father's

hands have trouble with his napkin,
which seems folded like some fluttering
white thing with wings.

AMY KNOX BROWN

Old Wives' Tales

Don't get your tit caught
in the wringer my mother warned
when she got wind I was courting trouble:
a late date; long whispered phone conversations;
times I waltzed in on a waft of smoke,
maybe drunk, maybe dazed from some activity
other than the movie
I was supposed to be seeing.

A wringer washer sat on Grandma's porch,
motorized, its rollers the tan of human flesh.
I'd seen them press tight together, suck clothes
through and crush moisture from material
while Grandma stood, hands on hips, watching
the machine jiggle and dance across the floor.

I never asked either of these women
if she'd known temptation, if she ever held
a licked finger against the iron's hot body
one instant after the hiss of spit
to understand pain, what it means
to go too far, to look too long
into a man's eyes, wait for that click

and dip toward him, as I do
and do. In the fresh press of flesh,
no space exists, but risk takes on a shape:
I hear my mother's warning, see
the slick cylinder of a wringer washer
that I have to navigate, leaning carefully
above the rollers, looking down into the tub
frothing and churning with soap, his old t-shirts,
and his wife's graying cotton brassieres.

J.V. Brummels

Dakota, 1933

Now, since the Corps
of Engineers built the bridge,
it's just across the river,
a fast Thursday night trip
to the university town's downtown slam,
perfect fit for four in a Cadillac,
headed to hear poets of another state
cuss the president by name
and list the long litany of his sins.

Back in the day
we crossed on the ferry,
an afternoon's gig.
While we waited
by the closed bar and bait,
the paddlewheeler struggled
across the current
of the only un-ditched stretch
this side of far Montana
toward our raised flag.

And when we ferried back
across the wide and wild water,
the pilot, back in country
just that year,
told of running off
the bribe-extorting Corpsman
with a .30-.30 from the wheelhouse.

More guns than poems then.

But it's the wind,
strong enough to flap a stiff hatbrim,
and the fifty-degree January night,
that makes tonight's trip historical,
the lead foot of climate change
accelerating this winter
through a coyote-killing cold November
to April showers in a month,
a pattern, I'm told, that apes
that year at the heart of dust.
Except for the age of the cars,
it could be South Dakota in '33,

a town named for a French color,
the color named for a western sky.

We pull in at sundown.
Some savage scent in the street air.
How hard must wind or war blow
before we begin to club
each other down in the streets?

Still, even after we ignite
the last of the world's gas,
this trip's only
a long, sunny winter day on a tall horse,
the wind watching our backs,
to cross the bridge
late beneath the stars
and ride toward what lights
the town has left.

And later, when all the dams
have silted in or washed out,
and that span too has crumbled,
a man—or some species—
will float us all
on a different ferry
just across the river
to the other side.

Shirley Buettner

Neighbor

By July the fields frame
my neighbor across the west section.

Her windows, so carefully Windexed,
flare and wink at me,

and from my back stoop I can see her
bent over her bean rows hoeing in

the night moisture. Soon the corn
throws up its green walls

covering the dark mouth of her house,
the nose, the eyes, and finally

the pale square hair of the roof.
Her wash flaps tearfully,

white handkerchiefs waving
goodbye, goodbye.

October

In a darkening October
the cottonwood trembles,
alive with a rabble
of blackbirds.

***

Swallows soar sideways
like Chinese kites
against wedges of light
that pull toward the south.

***

The maple, as it sheds brittle tones
of glowing brass and copper,

exposes neat bones
of empty nests.

***

While the crossbred dog barks
at his incessant echo,
the buck with mossed rack
lies down in quackgrass.

***

I hang husked puzzles
of Indian corn, carve grimaces
on the mouths of hollow men
whose heads burn with the inner fire
I have always asked for.

Michael Catherwood

The Cement Evangelical Worship Center

rises beyond the curve on south I-40,
looms above the dotted headlight fog at dusk.
As rush hour pushes its red eyes forward
onto exit ramps and into the wicked strip malls,
the concrete glares with its gray, conquering smirk.
Mud flaps of semis slap the godless wind.
On the hill Christ stands in cement sandals.

The worshipers must pray for electricity
to light up the fog; the chromed crucifixion atop
the steeple stares down I-240 East into the snake of traffic
blaspheming home. If someone in there shook
off sin, the rebar-enforced cement Jesus
might plod into Little Rock,
slouch into a bar and blast 3 shots of Bushmills,
plug old standards on the jukebox, 3 for a buck.

Someone glued shut the elaborate plastic doors
and disconnected the Amazing Grace doorbell.
In the gray powdery palms of Jesus, rust flows like rust
and the parched plastic flowers glare stoic,
barely move in these 40 mile-per-hour gusts.
Jesus stands in the fog, never complaining,
his gritty hands tired, the blood long gone.

JAMES CIHLAR

The Estate Auction

You asked me to go with you
to an estate auction thirty miles south.
I still can't get over your car:
late sixties Impala, rust-free,
big as a barge. You told me
about riding with your twin,
how you would lay your head
in his lap as he drove.
After I moved in, he would call
and leave messages like,
"Watch *Night Court,* it's funny."
We stopped at a Dairy Queen
on the way, probably the same one
I stopped at ten years later
with a student, on our way to a reading,
thinking how far away I'd gotten
from myself. Then we drove
through a town called Friend,
with the sign, "You've Got a Friend
in Friend." The auction was a bust,
tables of orange sunburst jewelry
and green pressed glass.
It was a chance to hold hands
in the car, I guess,
listen to the radio play "Precious and Few,"
like we did the night I told you
why I did not want to move in,
or like we did at the theater,
watching *Murphy's Romance,*
my jacket thrown over our hands.

Shelly Clark Geiser

My Daughter Picking Mulberries

That summer watching you scamper up Martha's tree like a monkey,
singing your little monkey song,
I yelled: not too high!
But already at eight you knew the secret of the climb.

Now, you tell me you hate me,
but I'm trying to keep count and it's not more times
than when you say you love me.

Your body, the body of a woman,
your breasts bounce a little in a skimpy black tank top
proclaiming in bright white letters: Bastard Sons of Johnny Cash.
You don't wave back, running across the lawn to jump into a car
driven by a boy straight out of reform school and the other one, he's not
even wearing a shirt.

The old junker sputters, coughs, peels off.
I try to see if your arms and hands might be moving
in the direction of a seat belt.

Back then, frightened, I yelled: Come down *now*.

And, you did, bucket of fruit plump and bursting,
your tiny hands
bloomed phlox.

The Zen of Goats

Lately,
I find myself doing things
out of the ordinary,

like stopping to watch the 4-H goats
at the Polk County Fair.

The judge is careful and
describes each one of them as if
they are unique and beautiful,
so I look at them

closer than I ever have,
and they are.

Even their swollen
udders, which look like
large pink melons straddled
between two spindly legs,
look strikingly exotic.

The judge points to the middle goat,
says she likes this one
because of its length of body,
says it is "very dairy." I love that
expression and could not have made it up.
"Very dairy."

The name of the goat is
Sherri TSM Belinda,
and her near-perfect rear udder attachment
is what puts her over the line,
Grand Champion!

But mostly, I am drawn to her
beady dark eyes, set perfectly in the triangle of her head,
as she looks out at us, so complacent,
so forgiving of her circumstances.

I lean into the metal bars of the goat pen
to get a better look,
as if by looking longer, loving more,
it will be easier to leave this world,
the goats of this world,
and the sweet smell of wind after rain.

Elizabeth Clark Wessel

Asylum

Swedish investigators are baffled by a mysterious illness affecting over 400 children of asylum-seekers, mostly from former Soviet and Yugoslav states, who fall into a deep depression and lose the will to live.
(REUTERS)

First the children stopped speaking.
No one noticed. Few understood their languages anyway.
They stared at the window

but saw neither window nor sky.
Nor heard the voices of the other children
laughing or sometimes crying but rarely silent.

At home there were calls in the darkest hours of the night.
Whispers between mothers and fathers
With more to worry about than quiet children.

When they stopped eating mother took it personally.
And now this? She said.
You know better. She said.

Eat. When we had nothing. Think of when we had nothing.

One day they stopped moving and lay all day in bed.
Water untouched. Food uneaten.

Mothers and fathers took them to a hospital,
A needle forced them to live.
People noticed. They got a name.

They faded into walls,
Into blankets, into the stale air around them.

They disappeared into their own nothingness.
They accused with their own nothingness.

People could hardly stand to look at them,
Those children who forgot everything.
Those children who saw everything and then didn't.

Marilyn Coffey

Pricksong

I am cursed
by a large penis
which I planted in a flower pot
in my living room.
When it grew, like a cactus,
it looked thirsty and,
being kindly at heart,
I allayed its thirst
with water. It sprouted wings.
Now it flies around the house
and sings at me.
Once I tried to shoot it down
but horrified, it shriveled up
into a ball, retracting everything
it had ever said to me. What
could I do? I didn't have the heart
to follow through. Now it tries to get
in bed with me. I am afraid.
It is so big. It looks so thirsty.
It is never satisfied. Last night
when I pushed it back, it cried.

Paul Dickey

Constellation

> *Nova Persie appeared in Perseus in 1901. For one night in February, it was the brightest star in the sky. By July it had almost disappeared, after which faint surrounding nebulous masses were discovered, apparently moving radially outward from the star at incredible velocity.*

At her sink, someone Ajaxes
last night's burnt moon.
Stars glitter from the spackled ceiling.

The sun rises through a kitchen window,
another 19" screen
that somehow always needs wiping.

When she was young, friends
orbited her.
She found men, taught them how to want.

In the living room, images are constant.
Electronic charges
aim bullets at purple nerves, promising

her press will hold through a thousand
washings. She would
hang the March rain out to dry,

if just this once tonight, it would make
him happy,
make the children stop circling.

Now the pans are half clean. Silver scars,
miniscule lightning,
in the dark morning of the kitchen.

MARILYN DORF

Dawn Watch

In depth
of quiet water

an old fish
feels its way

up toward
the morning

pushing darkness
away with its fins

its blue nose
nothing but a bow

of spun satin
resting for one

moment
on the thin line

water makes
on air

LORRAINE DUGGIN

Steamer Trunk

My Czech grandmother's trunk
contained her worldly goods,
memorabilia, treasures she couldn't
leave behind: embroidered
sheets, embossed pillowcases,
hand-stitched towels, lacy
crocheted scarves, quilts,
rugs braided, floral designs
woven into beauty
I've never seen, never
even heard about.

My father, eighty-five now,
depressed by a slowly-mending left hip,
tells stories he's never told,
tells me about the trunk,
stolen when he was four,
gone to Wisconsin with parents,
baby brother, for the winter,
seeing about some land,
trunk left behind
with care
instructions
a promise from neighbors.

Hard times, a world cast
adrift, Old Country grieved,
not missed, battlefield now,
new home, America
foreign as betrayal
empty shed, silent neighbors,
precious, tangible links,
family love
never passed on, never
seen again, handed down
never mentioned.

PAT HEMPHILL EMILE

Killings

for M. J. C.

The swing was red and the rope
was scratchy like Daddy's face.
I could touch the green leaves;
the wind made them dance.
Our house was white.
Mrs. Brinkman's chickens were white.
She held the stick with the shine.
The chickens' feet were yellow.
When she grabbed one,
it squawked and its feet ran
in the air. I went up high
and the shine came down
on the white chicken.
Its feet were red then. It wobbled
around her yard with its head off
and fell in the grass. She tied
its feet together and hung it
over the clothesline.
It rocked back and forth. The red
was on the green grass.
I stood on the swing
to make it go faster.

Kelly Madigan Erlandson

Nebraska

This is a place for things that take time. Long histories
that need to be unrolled and laid out across oak library tables,
with a hard-backed book set on each corner to keep them pressed open.
Here, we understand that shadows fold their wings and settle down
in midday, tucked underfoot like a coyote den the unschooled never
notice. We can see a fire in the next county, the smoke a thundercloud
of blackbirds twirling for fall, grouping and regrouping themselves
as though to remember something already lost, washed out
and splayed in the wet clay of the creek bed. You can drive
an entire afternoon here and not see a person, but all the way
the meadowlarks will be opening the doors of their throats,
letting out music like milkweed seeds delivered downwind.
You might start counting those birds after awhile, picture them
as mile markers on the telephone wires, wondering if you've seen
the same one over and over again. We have more stars here, so many
that strangers think there is something wrong with our sky, that it's
fake or that Sioux women have beaded our night with constellations
not seen in Minneapolis or Memphis, fresh ones that we can give
names to as we lie on the hood of the car. We can call one *Mountain
Lion Reclaims Ancestral Home*, after the cougar who roamed up
a wooded thicket into Omaha this fall, ranging until the zoo director
shot him with a tranquilizer dart. Here we can keep naming star puzzles
until the threat of sunrise blues the black space above us.
This is a place for things that take time, the long stitching together
of soft spots in the heart, the wind across the Missouri River Valley
scooping loess into hills unlike any others on this continent,
seeds stored in the cellar of the prairie for a hundred years
patient for fire, unable to crack themselves open without it.
This is a place where disappointments deep as aquifer
can spill themselves out, fill up and empty again, as many times
as the wound requires. This is a place where a person can heal,
or choose not to heal. We have both kinds.

Twenty-Five Years Later, She Learns Her Ex is Dying

Five nights in succession she recalled him in dreams.
His voice was a series of clicks and whistles,
the sound of Burlington Northern Santa Fe
troubling the long rails. If she starts to walk
those tracks, her cupboard doors will spill
their store of crackers and oats onto the floor,
her shingles slip from the sure grasp of the roof.
Linoleum plans to stall her. The dog knows
to sigh and paw the water bowl. Her climbing
rose has been positioning itself all summer.

Still, she remembers herself as a sundress
waving from a make-shift clothesline on the fire escape
of a red brick building. Or as a banner of blonde hair
advertising from the back of a black motorcycle.
She wants to take up cigarettes again, sleepwalk,
lose both shoes at a party in a neighboring town.
She wants to tell him something, or sing a chorus
of that old Donovan song to him, maybe just over
the phone. She remembers shuffling the Tarot cards,
intuiting a future much more wondrous than the thud
of news on her narrow porch, the civil greetings
penned to college friends. She wants something old,
something stolen. She wants to balance on that rail
as though she were not an owner of things, as though
the train were due, as though everything still mattered.

BECKY FABER

My Sister

My sister takes six baths a day,
not in a warm tub of scented salts
or prolific bubbles,
but in tepid water

She tells me that she is learning to swim,
something she feels she must do
before visiting either coast

She says that ignorance is not bliss

My sister chooses only friends whose first name begins with A—
Ann, Angie, Andy, Alan, Anthony (never Tony)

She says that she can only handle one letter at a time
and that these people understand
the concept of linear sequence
and how first things must come first

My sister always carries a photograph of the President
in her purse

She says that she admires his ability to lie,
how Pavlov has trained him to slobber untruths
on a daily basis

My sister says that life is easy to understand,
that the rest of us complicate it
with delusions & distractions & deconstructions

My sister says to start at the beginning,
be willing to admit what you don't know,
and always know the enemy

My sister wears a watch on each wrist,
one with a Mickey Mouse face and the other
with the face of Jesus

They are set for different time zones.
Either way,
she says,
time is not on our side

The Fisherman's Wife

She waits tables
at the Bayview Café,
de-mystifying the contents
of seafood chowder
for tourists

She tells me that her husband is
a fisherman,
asks where I am from,
sighs and says she has never been
west of Boston

She cannot imagine middle America,
a place without coastline,
a place where people eat beef daily

Each time she moves from table to kitchen,
I notice a different tattoo,
legs and arms twirling in color
like a globe

On long winter evenings
      I will eat chowder
      from a can

      The Maine fisherman with red,
      cracked fingers
      will trace each tattoo

      The fisherman's wife will close her eyes
      and tell him that he is
      all of the world
      that she needs

CHARLES FORT

The Vagrant Hours

September

The month of sonnets:
The long distance runners roamed the hills
recited their poems in the afternoon and kissed.
The poet-professor in corduroy cuffed pants
daydreamed of the evening flask of black whisky
his nights watch over the hour glass of metaphors.
The young men were cumbersome in their stalls.

October

The month of sestinas:
The charm of lovers against the burred ivy walls
held the riddle of sixes and coaxed the student's heart
to a blackboard of pentagrams and tarot flames in chalk.
The griot's basket of apples, chestnuts, and maple leaves
held back the screen door of their teacher's writing studio.
The young women were cumbersome in their shawls.

November

The month of villanelles:
The young poet nods off in the back of the classroom
and a wooden pointer curled the cowlick on his head.
He was made to stand before the assembly and sing.
With long shadows and wings of the runners on the hill
into November's end and the town clock's vagrant hour
he lowered his head and begged a rhyme scheme for love.

December

The month of elegies:
They held the widow's wreath and opulent arms of death
kissed the child's thumb that broke out of a wool mitten.
They waited under a rain of taps and six gun salute
for the son to place his hand on his father's cheek
for the wry minister to rise from his narrow chair
and place the widow's glove and ring in the tomb.

January

The month of blank verse:
They say he tracked a wounded animal
drop for drop for three and a half damn weeks
broke its long neck bare handed dead and stirred
right strong coffee until he heard noises.
The hot prairie wind howled a fancy tune.
He knew it was a way of knowing things.

February

The month of ballads and woe:
The traveler brings a small gift to her screen door
and he barely remembers the song she whispered
sixteen years before under the lilac covered bridge.
Was that her low voice rising above the top of trees
or a meteor with its own articulation of the heavens
in the arc of falling embers that filled the brown field?

March

The month of pantoums:
She stood for hours in mud
for a handsome young man
who turned into a beer slug
not a fine bottle of wine.

For a handsome young man
who turned into a beer slug
not a fine bottle of wine
she stood for hours in mud.

April

The month of odes and affliction:
This was not the cruelest nor a tepid month Mr. Eliot
until a letter arrived out of nowhere from a best friend
the best damned drinking friend twenty six years ago.
He wrote about old poems that spent his failing heart
who had very little time in the red stained hour glass
how he was on a waiting list for love and a new heart.

May

The month of heroic couplets:
Let there be thunder in his heart again
let a church bell's echo dance in his pen!
Where he erred once let him live twice
as he lived once let him sing with light
Let his hands turn the hour glass
and the last sailboat raise its mast!

June

The month of pastorals:
The poet met Art Pierce cliff side at *Ojo Caliente*
his calligraphy on clay birds in mosaic and arsenic
sent by the god of letters to the underworld spring.
They lifted their chalices to the crippled and mortal
who swam the miracle waters for the unkind rebirth
who sought refuge in the ghost chamber of the earth.

July

The month of stanzas:
This was the month of writer's block.
Nothing moved his fingers on the typewriter
until rain outside his studio in the burnt sky
formed a rainbow in the watchmaker's eyepiece.
What landed on his bad shoulder a poor white raven
found in his good hand a ruby from the baker's oven.

August

The month of open forms in his bare hands:
The poet learned *the rules of the dance*
in the black ink spread across the pages
one misspelled word in the spelling bee.
He studied the burial ground of images
how love was subtle and hidden in a line
how love was metered and love was rare.

Tom Gannon

Bird Poem

in the high black hills of south dakota
you can tell the piñon jay from the blue jay
by the yack of its phony french accent

here, too, the wheeze of the pine siskin
betrays to a blind man the browner bird
among its goldfinch cousins

and as for the silence—well, that could be
either a great horned owl in flight,
or just that—the silence

the thing is in the approach, to come into a clearing
with the green awe of an eight-year-old, youth-
fevered, on the back of his first shetland

there is nothing better than to hear nothing at all,
and then the plain, sure notes of a chickadee
right there off to your left, in that stand of yellow pines

to know the birds, you need to know
their native idioms, the rise and fall
of a peculiar cadence in the sounds they make—
the rest is, as they say, a matter of technique

Bird Poem II

a junco must be a quiet one
when the dark shell comes, must
close eyes, wings against the cold

then white light breeze—up to sing can sing
andsingcansingand thank the thawed
brink of a puddle for a quick drinkandsing

down to hard snow ground for scattered
seed singand seed singandseed and
back to the hard snow pine to sing thanks sing

as the white light breeze slightens,
less busy—preen a wing—last burst of
sing—until all soft, and still, and warm

then a junco must be silent
when the dark shell comes, then i must
close my eyes; my wings; against the cold

GAYNELL GAVIN

Identification

I have to believe she didn't lie
when she pointed him out and the judge
intoned, *Let the record reflect*
the witness has pointed to the defendant.

Here, have this image:
a round scar burnt like a third eye
in the middle of a slight, brown man's
forehead. She'd described her rapist:
a large very black man. She mentioned no scar.

I believe she needed to believe
they'd caught the right man
as I need to believe
I didn't understand what I saw.
True, I've failed to tell much,
say to give a picture
of the black-robed judge.
I could give him a name, like Sparky
Jenkins, The Honorable Sparky Jenkins.
I don't remember his name.

I don't remember the girl—
nondescript, light brown hair
like mine—only the scar
and that prosecutor back at the office,
laughing, *God, he looked like Cyclops.*
Can you believe that judge gave us
a conviction when that girl
didn't even mention the scar?
That prosecutor later ran
for some public office. She'd say
I'm crazy and made this up.
I'm too tired to make this up.

Military Secrets

His mother and I, encoded with warnings before we
dream he'll want to fly; great dark eyes, brown-
gold curls, he crawls across light on hardwood.
We blink into sunlight. He finishes college,
huge, strong, taller even than his tall father, head shaved,

face lean; eyes dark bright stars shine above me. I look
up into them—he looks like my son—his smile so beautiful,
who could not love him? We invade Iraq. The helicopter pilot has
a secret life. Barely a speck, I am almost nothing on the world's
radar screen. A friend says, *We believe in God because we have to*

believe in something better than ourselves. I live among skeptics,
and who can blame them, but were our sons' bodies ever really so
small they fit inside our own? Each day, and at night, awake,
remembering I carried the pilot on one hip, I say, God, give
me this pilot. I knew him before he took his first steps.

S. C. Hahn

Great Uncle Louie

Uncle Louie stood impregnable
against besiegers of his ordered world
under his dark tower of porkpie hat,
his eyes armored black with horn-rimmed glasses
from which he scoured horizons near and far,
his clip-on bow-tie tilted like a vat
of oil over the white shirt's curving wall,
buttoned suspenders that hefted his cuffed pants
out of the reach of flood, famine or fire,
and his shoes (bought half-price every other winter)
were gray behemoths sheathed in steel-toed leather,
bound with lashes running through shiny eyelets.
And Uncle Louie, poker-faced to the last,
joked that death would never take him alive.

Snow on Far Mountain

The elderberry's blossoms will melt in summer
but now they pile in drifts reaching the top
of that little jade mountain, where an ant
climbs in a coat lacquered black with rain.

In classic Japanese woodcuts, one often meets
a man—a poet, perhaps—whom age has bent
like elderberry branches. His cloak might be blue,
tinged with the gray of some long-reconciled sadness
and beyond him glimmers turquoise sky, same hue
as a river far below from where he has walked,
and his sash is heavy with dark berries printed on silk.

The mountain on which he climbs is hummocked with snow
in spite of the summer season, but it is unclear
whether he is merely out for a morning stroll
and is catching his breath, seeking nothing more
than the yellow moss on that stone; whether he shall ever
stand on the peak and look back down at his life;
or whether he will lie down in the shade that crosses
his path like a bridge, to rise again only as water.

Twyla Hansen

Late Winter: Survival

First, attempt to describe the blackbirds, the plentiful
anonymous mass in the top of the cottonwood.

Begin with "black," "copious" and "red-winged," knowing
that anything specific will point only to more uncertainty.

They will perch there, noisy and prim, defying also
narration. Your mouth will be slack, your neck craned.

In the *Populus*, meaning prevalent, meaning of little
ornamental value, the tree that grew like a weed.

Forget the Canadian breeze, the chill that knuckles
your resolve, the snow deeper than recent memory.

It will bring to mind those monster drifts of old days,
how you and your brother climbed into the heights

of the shelterbelt, slid later into muck, the farmstead
and roads and countryside a sea of endless mud,

until summer, when the wind exhaled, the soil cracked
and you ached for rain. Oh, my child, how you dreamed!

And now this cackling confusion of starlings overhead,
the sun at a sharper angle, rousing the earth.

Not the songbirds you smile at, but a migrating pack
that grows darker with each passing day. Right now

the earth is tilted just so and the sunlight is brilliant
and everything, every last thing seems possible.

Potato Soup

In the early years she helped her mother plant peels,
carry the dishpan out to the garden, digging holes.

What you eat is what you plant, her mother always said,
that edible tuber common as dirt, a near-daily staple.

One grandmother left potato country long ago for this one,
another immigrated for the promise of more potato land.

As she learned to cook, she began peeling alone at the sink,
sticking a spare slice on her tongue, smell of starch

lingering on her fingers. Mashed, fried, baked on Sundays
for hours, regular as pulsating winds over the plains.

Soon graduating to French fries in sizzling grease, to fermented
spirits of the potato. Beginning with a certain look in an eye,

relying on folklore, that time of the month safe if planted
at night under the expansive and unblinking moon. Grabbling

into the soil around roots to steal an eager potato or two.
She's fond of the skin color, the flesh, textures, exotic flavors.

Moving on to potato-salad years, quick-boiled varieties
from the hot tub. Decades here and gone; potato-love constant.

By now she's concluded it's best on gradual simmer, consolation
accompanying maturity. In the afternoon she sautés onion

and butter, stirs in flour and milk, chops celery, carrot, adds
chicken stock. She thinks of the hour when they'll be eating,

into twilight, of the long night ahead in front of the fire.
Should she throw in something extra, for tang, for play—

a measure of chardonnay? All her life, she thinks, it has come
down to this, bringing the bottle up slow to meet her lips.

We Are On Nine-Mile Prairie When

the news reaches us of twin towers and collapse,
walking with fourth-graders through tall grass,
our guide uttering bluestem and goldenrod, mammal
and snake, this early report not yet registering,

the sun high, burning. Standing on the unplowed,
the whole, no broken sod or surreal debris, only silence,
learning pollination and forb, coyote and mouse,
deer and split-hoof adaptation. This unspoiled place

a split screen—reels replaying later—spider and insect,
growth points above or below, roots with tentacles deeper
than imagination. How do we comprehend fanatics? Out here
we speak French—*prairie*: treeless meadow, evolving

through the millennia. Plant, animal, weather intertwined,
on each other dependent. The first people and fire, following
the source. Fourth grade, when school grows more complex,
when the curriculum includes heritage. How do we define

fear, the future, the dead? The blameless children, rabbits,
bolt from predators, crouch in grass. Nowhere to run, nowhere
to hide, no superman to reverse the earth's rotation, start
this day over. Wings in the air, the claws of terror. We pause

on thatch in the brief quiet, breathe unsullied air. While
winds blow our way, we search for words, phrases,
language that is truly alive. Are we safe on this, our only,
planet? Each child becoming the smallest prey.

9-11-01

NEIL HARRISON

Naming the Lakes

Sometimes at night a younger world awakes,
sounds and scents and scenes I'd long forgotten,
and I can hear Olga naming the lakes—

Hackberry, Dewey, the Alkali Lakes,
Watts, Duck, Rice, Dad's, Schoolhouse and Pelican.
Sometimes at night a summer world awakes

with Ernest telling me to watch for snakes
mornings on the Rosebud reservation,
where I can hear Olga naming the lakes

we plan to fish—He Dog, Beed's—as she makes
coffee, French toast, scrambled eggs and bacon.
Sometimes at night a somber world awakes,

vast concrete dams flood the Missouri breaks
for miles above Pierre, Ft. Randall, Yankton,
and I can hear Olga naming the lakes—

Gavin's, Oahe—and those long blue aches
ring true in the gray light of that false dawn,
those times at night when the grave world awakes
and I can hear Olga naming the lakes.

ART HOMER

Turkey Vultures

*The majority of the Universe - some 70% - is composed of
dark energy, an equally mysterious quantity which exerts
negative pressure.*
        from *"Team Finds Proof of Dark Matter"*
        —BBC News Service

Given wind enough these big birds
go acrobat, six foot plus of wing,
negative space against the years first
thunderheads southwest.
                        Barrel roll,
stall turn, everything short of loop.
Migrate by maintaining stall against
prevailing wind, wait a week for sun
and bloat to cook your meat, and you'd
stand on one wing in the face of storms
that emit lightning and a galaxy of cloud
and homeowners, pulling their sheets
off lines, colliding with their own
trash and patio furniture, the pulverized
receipts of dead deals blown from offices
of seed salesmen, cabs of grain trucks.
Vultures must absorb light, draggled stars
parked on snags and fence posts till the dew
evaporates from wing and back, must launch
themselves into thick air while blackbirds
and kingbirds strafe their bald grey pates.
Safe in the updrafts, they maintain their
septic orbit over the bluffs. I watch them
for the good news: uplift.
                        Let the field sparrows'
cries rebound, the bluebirds and the cardinals
rejoice. Gouts of empty space, the vultures wheel
above them, lenses through the false blue
to all that lies beyond. What does the dark
matter if they are not afraid? Clouds gather
themselves unto themselves until we cannot
read their intent or direction. Safe in wind,
they know that clinging to the earth
is the surest way to be pulled apart.

Don Jones

Thousands at His Bidding Post

He dreamed that he delivered
      a letter to himself
          and came to the door
and held the letter out
      and reached for it
          and took it.
What it said
      as he carried on
          on the route unknowing
what it said
      as he opened it
          by the picture window snowing
what it said
      was a blank page—
          no way of ever knowing
who had sent it
      or just why
          unless the way
the way he had delivered
      a letter to himself
          was in the mind of God
where resident
      and postman
          are as one as one
hand warms
      the other on the man
          now blotted out by snow.

William Kloefkorn

Connections: A Toast

Here's to the bur oak, *Quercus macrocarpa*, rising
just beyond my office window, here's to window,
to oxide and silicon, to their joining, here's to joining,
to fusion, pro and con, to transparency
that brings to the eye Renoir:
two young students, woman and man,
transecting the campus, here's to transecting, here's to
campus, over their shoulders bookbags no doubt containing
books, here's to books, *Gray's Anatomy*, perhaps,
let's hear it for Gray, let's hear it for anatomy, and

maybe something for Aeschylus or Plato, here's to Plato,
and while we're at it here's to Socrates,
to the goblet he raised to toast those immortal
kissing cousins, inquiry and innovation, here's to kissing,
to cousins, to inquiry and innovation, and perhaps
at the bottoms of the bags some thoughts
from Augustine or Jung, saint and otherwise,
here's to saint, here's to otherwise, Jung who said
*It is not Goethe who creates Faust, it is Faust
who creates Goethe,* here's to Goethe and Faust,

to a myriad of bone-and-brain creations,
to the act that marks each beginning,
to the moment whose enemy is stasis,
to the runner on first with stealing on his mind,
here's to the stolen base, the purloined kiss,
here's to motion perpetual, here's to mind, to flesh,
to the hitter at the plate, Jackie Robinson,
to the man on deck, Pee Wee Reese, to the hotdogs
in the box seats, to the peanuts in the gallery,
to Ebbets Field and Fenway Park and to Rosa Parks
who refusing to ride side-saddle
becomes a blue-chip conscientious ob-jec-tor—*There
is some waste I will not eat*—so here's to Rosa Parks,
to side, to saddle, here's to the horse
beneath the saddle, to sound horse and to Crazy Horse
whose hemlock was the feel of a cold bayonet,
whose words were prayer because they were not meant
as prayer—*It does not matter where this body
lies, for it is grass; but where this spirit is, there
it will be good for all of us to be*—and to the bird

with its coat of many colors, bird now perched
on the topmost branch of the bur oak, *Quercus macrocarpa,*

trilling now Bach, now Beethoven, now Louis Armstrong,
trilling, with its unsplit tongue, one
steady and diverse and universal song.

My Love for All Things Warm and Breathing

I have seldom loved more than one thing at a time,
yet this morning I feel myself expanding, each
part of me is soft and glandular, and under my skin
is room enough now for the loving of many things,
and all of them at once, these students especially,
not only the girl in the yellow sweater, whose
name, Laura Brighton, is somehow the girl herself,
Laura for the coy green mellowing eyes, Brighton
for all the rest, but also the simple girl in blue
in the back row, her mouth sad beyond all reasonable
inducements, and the boy with the weight problem,
his teeth at work even now on his lower lip, and
the grand profusion of hair and nails and hands and
legs and tongues and thighs and fingertips and
wrists and throats, yes, of throats especially,
throats through which passes the breath that joins
the air that enters through these ancient windows,
that exits, that takes with it my own breath, inside
this room just now my love for all things warm and
breathing, that lifts it high to scatter it fine and
enormous into the trees and the grass, into the heat
beneath the earth beneath the stone, into the
boundless lust of all things bound but gathering.

Bruce Koborg

Army of One

I am an Army of One.

I go, where you don't wanna go,

and I clean up the messes caused in the name

of your comfort.

I make less than minimum wage,

and I operate on less than minimum sleep.

I don't get to hide in an undisclosed location.

I have only hot and stinky body armor between me,

and 120 pissed off people who want their lights

back on,

in 120 degree heat,

as I pack 120 pounds of gear

to lug around, because I'm in somebody else's home,

not my own.

I am an Army of One.

I am the Captain Willard and Colonel Kurtz inside every

19 year old American, and my methods are 'unsound'.

I should be in class now,

but I got orders to make the world safe for Spring Break.

My ass is chafed, my body armor smells like a giant shoe,

and we're down to one MRE a day, so back off.

I'm surrounded by some kids who take soccer balls that we hand out, and some

kids who drive trucks at our checkpoint and then

laugh at us when we lock and load on them

as they turn away at the last second.

I can't tell which is which.

They don't want me here.

I don't want me here.

I want to be stateside,

I want air conditioning,

I want cold beer and a hot shower.

I am an Army of One.

I have nothing to say to you when I get back,

because you won't understand,

or care.

When I get back, you won't want me there,

because I'll remind you of something that you'd

rather forget.

Ted Kooser

At the Cancer Clinic

She is being helped toward the open door
that leads to the examining rooms
by two young women I take to be her sisters.
Each bends to the weight of an arm
and steps with the straight, tough bearing
of courage. At what must seem to be
a great distance, a nurse holds the door,
smiling and calling encouragement.
How patient she is in the crisp white sails
of her clothes. The sick woman
peers from under her funny knit cap
to watch each foot swing scuffing forward
and take its turn under her weight.
There is no restlessness or impatience
or anger anywhere in sight. Grace
fills the clean mold of this moment
and all the shuffling magazines grow still.

Etude

I have been watching a Great Blue Heron
fish in the cattails, easing ahead
with the stealth of a lover composing a letter,
the hungry words looping and blue
as they coil and uncoil, as they kiss and sting.

Let's say that he holds down an everyday job
in an office. His blue suit blends in.
Long days swim beneath the glass top
of his desk, each one alike. On the tip
of each morning, a bubble trembles.

No one has seen him there, writing a letter
to a woman he loves. His pencil is poised
in the air like the beak of a bird.
He would spear the whole world if he could,
toss it and swallow it live.

Selecting a Reader

First, I would have her be beautiful,
and walking carefully up on my poetry
at the loneliest moment of an afternoon,
her hair still damp at the neck
from washing it. She should be wearing
a raincoat, an old one, dirty
from not having money enough for the cleaners.
She will take out her glasses, and there
in the bookstore, she will thumb
over my poems, then put the book back
up on its shelf. She will say to herself,
"For that kind of money, I can get
my raincoat cleaned." And she will.

So This is Nebraska

The gravel road rides with a slow gallop
over the fields, the telephone lines
streaming behind, its billow of dust
full of the sparks of redwing blackbirds.

On either side, those dear old ladies,
the loosening barns, their little windows
dulled by cataracts of hay and cobwebs
hide broken tractors under their skirts.

So this is Nebraska. A Sunday
afternoon; July. Driving along
with your hand out squeezing the air,
a meadowlark waiting on every post.

Behind a shelterbelt of cedars,
top-deep in hollyhocks, pollen and bees,
a pickup kicks its fenders off
and settles back to read the clouds.

You feel like that; you feel like letting
your tires go flat, like letting the mice
build a nest in your muffler, like being
no more than a truck in the weeds,

clucking with chickens or sticky with honey
or holding a skinny old man in your lap
while he watches the road, waiting
for someone to wave to. You feel like

waving. You feel like stopping the car
and dancing around on the road. You wave
instead and leave your hand out gliding
larklike over the wheat, over the houses.

Greg Kosmicki

Windows

Which is easier, to say
"Your sins are forgiven you,"
or to say, "Rise, and walk?"

Luke

At my office the new cube
I moved into has a brick wall
on one side and no windows.
I am not terribly unhappy here
just desperate. Desperate for something,
something that is not
on the computer screen. Something
trees, and wind. I've noticed
the reflection of the fluorescent
ceiling lights makes two little
window-like pictures on my screen
when my computer has what the
computer people call the "desktop"
showing—no desktop at all
of course, like everything else
on the computer, it's virtual—
a simulation of whatever's
there. The reflections of the lights
are real and the smears
from my fingertips—one looks like
a head, almost, a silhouette,
but all the rest of them look
like clouds, the effect
heightened by the fact
that the fluorescent's bluish
color against the green
quote unquote desktop
makes the reflection, real
as it is, a blue sky blue,
a cerulean virtual sky
like looking through a window
in the roof. It might look like
the hole that Jesus saw
when those desperate friends
of that desperate man
lowered him to the healer

through the hole they'd broken
in the roof. Who does that
make me like? Jesus, or the sick man
lying on his pallet in his rags,
lowering slowly down into
the midst of the crowd,
gripping the sides of his cot
like a man destined for
greatness or agony? I know
I am not the healer,
I must be the paralyzed man
and that makes more sense—
for here am I
not in my body
before the computer.
So I let myself be lowered
and each time I fall
on rags held by my friends
into the presence
of the one who can heal,
I look up and see
the sky, sky so azure
it breaks my heart,
clouds like fingertips of rain,
and fall into that healing sky lost
somewhere, out on a prairie
by an abandoned grade, boxcars
of sky clanking past, a two car
train filled with sky,
my fingerprint clouds holding
the sky inside together, yellow
buttercups, daisies
tall grass, wind, and I lie
here on this floor, meadowlarks
calling to me the world's first name.

Greg Kuzma

Let There Be An End to Excuses

When you are old and defeated and your elbows
protrude from your clothes like so many drunken
football fans, say you are learning from experience
the price of victory. When you are old, and your
few teeth are your last few friends, say it is OK
there is more room now in your mouth for your
tongue, where before there was never enough
space to echo its fine speeches. When you are old,
and your skin bags on you like trousers on the
clothesline in the wind, say rather that beauty is
not skin deep, and that some major preoccupation
with obscure studies has kept you from marrying the
girl of your choice. And when you are old, and
the lights are dim in both your eyes, and your
eyeglasses are heavy as barbells, and your hands
are brown and twisted as dead wasps, say instead
of the usual "I count the days" that you are ready,
to deal the cards, to put the pot on, to call time
out so that you can come back into the game.

Sometimes

Sometimes I feel like the girl who goes along,
who is not pretty, who is somehow a best friend
to the heroine, who is not loved, who is afraid
of snakes and spiders, but who goes into the jungle
with the rest, and who, straying from the camp
one night, hearing something no one else does,
is attacked by terrible creatures that swarm about
her head, and which she does not at first take
seriously. She starts swatting them, thinking
they are merely mosquitoes, and just about the
time it becomes obvious to us all and to her that
this is it, and her helpless flailings cripple us
in our seats as we watch, the scene shifts to the
two lucky ones in their tent, wrapped in each other's
arms, who hear, faintly in the distance, the afflicted
screaming, but who for now will be spared this thing
that is coming. There is, of course, an arrogance
to my identification here, that I should somehow be

crucial to the plot, that I should have senses
beyond the normal so that I am drawn toward things
others don't notice, and that I might be, in some
situations, though painfully, the first to know.

When We Dead Awaken

My father was a blacksmith without a forge.
He died without a forge,
but having made everything in his life
with his own hands,
the earth he went into was like a brother to him,
although he was much afraid.

Someday when the dead awaken
he will rise with them
and they will all come forth
to sit at all the chairs and tables
they have abandoned,
so strong was their pain
that they had got up from our tables
and gone off searching for the end of it.

Oh there is a day
(and I feel it may be soon)
when we the few stragglers left
must go down to the ground
never to walk across the yard again
in the afternoon
never to dress for the party
admire outselves in the mirror
never to kiss the sweet mouths
of our children
in the mornings, Sundays,
with no work to go to.

It is said that the dead will awaken
and the living with them
all those among us and including even
ourselves
who have lived our lives as if asleep
and all our eyes will open
on the world
and we will gasp in pleasure at the sight
and the breath from our lips

will nearly extinguish the sun
and all life's vanities
will come to an end
but I do not believe it.

STEVE LANGAN

Meet Me at the Happy Bar

In this corner, blood on a shawl,
and in that corner, representative man.

A bluebird dead on the hillside.
 "*Bluebird*" or "blue bird"?

And how to describe its splayed plumage,
beak tipped in mud,
beneath the yellow-x'd oak?

Excess as a strategy against our dying?

After you finish your project,
will you meet me at the Happy Bar?

Moody interrogations or awestruck reminiscences?

"Somewhat closer to the heart of experience than usual,
but still not close enough"
is Paul Klee's epitaph.

Daylight's twittering details, as if from the broken jaw
of a parakeet.

(Nevertheless, one eventually tires
of the "talking component.")

(And seeing as you divulged it,
now your pet bird begs you by name for *water*.)

—A way to make the dust stop
in its descent under light, the mind
connecting some objects in the sitting room,
embracing some, rejecting others?...

Or a ritual involving "talking into a megaphone
at the sunblazed boatyard"
made exquisite, like a dollar postcard, by *leaving*?

Notes on Landscape

The landscape—this new landscape—resolving itself.

No more than four of you on that side of the picnic table
or it'll topple over.

He's a little guy, just a speck of grease and noise.

Born to stroll in quiet weather, just looking around.

In his old loafers with crust on his lips.

Swirling trajectories, remembered sciences, ultimatums.

This day's composite: nipple, bowl, spoon...

Some boys have gathered in the storefront light.

With a mind of winter, one is looking at a looking-glass.

One is smoking, one is pacing,
and the synchronized breathing of the others.

Adequate strut, mean visage, distribution of fierceness.

It's the barometric pressure;
it's an affliction of the inner ear.

I handed you a packet of rice to throw at the moon.

After you tied iron and silver to the daring bride's car.

Along the way, singing and telling many lies.

Hurling our pain from the sidewalk into windows left open.

Every action in its rhythm, hallelujah, set us free!

Each excruciating blade of grass in its rhythm.

And the wind, too, regardless of what you have heard.

There goes a rat, past a fresh puddle of drool.

Salvation is a mouth with fine hair on its gums.

There is no other way but the sky. Focus.

There is no other way but the ridge. Listen.

The sun is pounding its fists at the low-flying birds.

Who are unbecoming to the rain-devouring roses.

With fish of all kinds curling up to die at the tide-line.

Ninety degrees today, could be a hundred tomorrow!

Pictures of miscarriages float past, a highlight reel
of devastations.

I swear I'll be home as soon as I wipe down the bar.

Only answer to our "secret-knock-with-the-doorknocker."

A horse slowly comes out of the trees,
a patch of mud under its left eye.

I have warned you about walking by yourself
out there.

I know it's a *drawing* of a horse but its mane looks
so real.

I must have told you a thousand times not alone.

Crickets

They call our names in the night,
inviting us into the middle air
where the wolf chews stars to pulp,
paws of stone resting on the emptied dream.
As we approach, the crickets retreat,
their song ringing like scars.
We pass the pumpkins rocking on vines,
the barn running, its arms full of boards.
Beyond the creek tattooed with minnows
is the oracle of flung seeds,
the staked earth between glass trees,
the ferns blackjacked from behind.
The raccoon opens a suitcase of bees.
The fox nudges the rabbit into the transept.
Robed with berries, the bear stands upright,
turns on a peg-leg, admonishing,
and departs with all our memories,
the piety of terror
padding the walls of the clearing.
As quail lift in blank escape,
fenceposts put steel shot in their pockets,
and everything shimmers,
the tear-shell room where laughter is born,
the sulphur lockets where love is stored,
the voyage of mercies and milk-cry,
the witch-breath balance of body
where the deaths on both sides
of our life are even,
where the years of pain, given and received,
are brushed with the oil of the moon.
Under the sapphire window the cat curls
on the slope of the cellar door.
They call our names in the night,
and leap and scurry above bandaged straw,
the last rumpus of the season,
the float of this crooked month
in the marrow of the unsaid year.

The Theory of Evolution

They were the meanest cats
I've ever seen, all snarl
and wheeze of distemper,
pus-eyed, ears chewed,
whiskers askew,
sandburs clotted in dirty fur.
Born wild in my uncle's barn
they stayed wild.
I never saw one asleep or playful,
or saw a kitten—they showed up
full grown, with a bad past.
They prowled between the barn
and the windmill like a street gang,
usually seven or eight of them.
The dog kept his nose,
which never healed properly,
in his own business.
Watching them on my visits to the farm
as a kid, I envied
their freedom and swagger,
the way they accepted
a pan of milk like protection money.
After the first mouse
was dragged across the ruts of the farmyard,
tossed and taunted,
and finally torn apart,
the mice in the granary
chose suicide,
gobbling up pellets of poison
or placing their necks
neatly on the trigger of the trap.
A coyote would get one
now and then,
but it was a fair fight.

MORDECAI MARCUS

Always Back There

Most of it is about fifty years back.
Start in the hobo jungles.
Over the mulligan stew a harmonica plays.
The railroad bulls don't haunt this territory.
The young and middle-aged travel together
towards points of further restlessness.
Fights leave brief scars, shapeless bruises;
rarely is a woman's taken body
struck with more than a farewell kiss.
Corpses in the ditches come from the sick and aged.

The songs! Well, yes, the songs! The songs don't stamp and scream.
The songs sway. The songs bring palm trees into your room.
In the songs you are drifting down the bay under a true blue moon.
The songs bring you what we are all waiting for.

And the streets. Well, yes, the streets are cold in winter and hot in summer.
But in the theaters' depths, warmth is cradled or fans blow the sweat away
and the screens are the truest silver that ever gleamed.
We walk right up before the screens and put ourselves down
to hear the sweet-tough talk we can never quite make our own,
and that is why the heroes stay heroes—gritty as clay
and sharp as blades. Bogey holsters his gun and pulls down the shades
and that's sweeter than any flashy display of breasts or thighs.
Garfield brushes off the roadside dirt and pushes on
bravely, as we all must. And there's Edward G.
talking tough because that's how one faces the world's ways
and how could we sweeten our smiles without the jest of such sourness?
Sylvia Sidney, Barbara Stanwyck, and Joan Blondell
are there to stand up for us and lie down when the last light fades
and we go separately home to our sparsely set tables.

Elsewhere, across the seas, Mr. Hitler is ranting and raving.
But since Mr. Hitler is mostly against the Communists and the Jews and the Poles
and since it's very far away, we don't need to worry—much.
Back home, the city corners bristle with panhandlers and soapbox speakers,
while in the great open lands the farmers stare at the skies and streams.
The wheat returns and the floods are dammed and the boys
are ripening for the thrills of a time for soldiers.

Seekers

Lear's Fool, seeing Gloucester approach with a torch,
said: "Look, here comes a walking fire."
He was right, bitterly right.
That fire paid the price of its aimlessness.
Soon, it sputtered and died, only a little wiser.

Freud, thinking perhaps of marble and of words, declared:
The ancients glorified the instinct, we the object.
Almost always—bitterness aside—his aim was truth.

But what shape can the glory of instinct take
besides the shapelessness of fire?
And how can the preciousness of flesh
be called "object," except by an Olympian
who needed words of ice to bear his own tenderness
in face of the naked vision
he rightly prized over all weaker kindnesses?

It is hard to tell if he was right about them and us.
He held up many torches, some sparks sputtered, others caught fire.
But sometimes truth is so hard that any softening will melt it.

To glorify the instinct is to live in a terrible isolation
To glorify the object is to live in a terrible isolation

(Whose lives were most frantic, whose most calm?)

Perhaps it was his dream to occupy the middle
with an army that kept changing into phantoms.

Clif Mason

Big Muddy

for Fredrick Zydek

I want to be this great river,
always emptying itself of itself,
recognizing twin dirt-and-shale banks
as its only limits;
galloping, a herd of bison, between,
shaking noses and big bosses
of dusky green water;
lying down in its long bed
to watch wind-whiffled clouds
drift between earth and moon and stars,
its head full of catfish and carp and gar,
sturgeon and walleyes and northerns—
full of scaled or plated
or stringy-whiskered thoughts;
with golden eagles and baldies roosting
on the big-branched cottonwoods
shading its face and lank, naked thighs.
Endlessly beset, hungry, angry to know—
what can we ever know
of our own depths and dangers:
smelling of dankness, humus, and fish,
with wheeling, snagging, eel-rooted elms,
barkless and branchless;
the safe, slow-flowing edge waters
and then the fast, shifting central channel,
with its deceitful under-currents
that grasp
with a strangler's dominating hands;
the sudden sharp drop-
offs, when one's feet walk, churning,
of an instant on water, under water?

The Old Crow

Even in full moonlight
I cannot see
the old crow
in the tree at night,
head tucked under a wing.
Yet I know it is there,
a blackness
robed in blackness.

MATT MASON

The Good News

> "Tell the good news about Jesus"
> —a bumper sticker I followed for a long time

Jesus lent me ten bucks when I forgot my wallet at lunch.
Sure, he could've ordered a chicken pesto sandwich
and broke it into two full meals, but he's no showoff.
That's what I like about Jesus.

Jesus listens to cool music. If it weren't for Jesus,
I never would have known about Tom Waits
or Ani DiFranco, and I sure wouldn't own any Lyle Lovett CDs.
But Jesus makes a kickass mix tape.

Jesus loves cows,
thinks my poems with cows in them are a hoot
and encourages me
to look at herds of white cows
in a green field
and imagine salvation
is underneath each windmill.

Jesus tells me Pat Robertson's right,
and so is Al Sharpton.
That they're both wrong, too,
but that's not the point.
His point is how God is sewn into every fabric.
Even yourself. Even Elvis.

Jesus saves and Jesus recycles.

Jesus eats fish for more
than Omega-3 fatty acids,
drinks red wine for more reasons
than his sacred heart.

Jesus doesn't dress like the Medieval paintings
with the gold hats and the Mr. T rosaries.
Sure, he can clean up nice,
but Jesus likes blue jeans.

Jesus makes a killer chianti,
but he refuses to turn water
into Diet Coke for me.
"What's the difference?" he asks.

Jesus pisses me off
with his honesty
sometimes.
But it's not like he's ever wrong.

Jesus acts real serious
when somebody rushes up to him hollering, "Jesus,
take me up to Heaven,
I will see you in the Kingdom, Jesus!"
Jesus says they should get their kumbayayas off
by putting on some overalls
and hammering in the morning:
may as well make Heaven bigger,
not just your ego.

Jesus digs the "How does Jesus eat M&M's" joke.
He won't do it at a party, but he did do it once
when just the two of us were watching cartoons.

Jesus wanted me to tell you he loves you.
Jesus also wants you to stop doing that thing.

Jesus tells me I'm saved.
Then he laughs real loud.
I hate it when Jesus does that.

JANELLE MASTERS

The Body

The little boy's body is so much
like his dad's body when they walk
they almost lean into each other,
lanky, shoulders wide, legs that just
keep unspooling. Bodies like that
are too angular for football, you
can see how the bones would break
hitting, hitting so hard. And the dad
has never been rough with the boy
or even tickled him too hard, the dad
says it's painful when you can't get
away and you're laughing and can't
get away and whoever it is on you
thinks it's okay—you're laughing
and you can't help it. So they walk,
with backpack and binoculars, voices
unreeling, what's that, what's that?
That looks like sourdough, the boy
says and the dad laughs because he
means sourdock, that tall weed
—the boy means. The boy remembers
what his dad tells him and the dad
doesn't fudge on what clouds are,
what causes rain, either. No it just
comes from God, son, but how it
comes, the finger of God in the drop
of rain. And now the dad is gone
and the mother thinks of how
they told her the boy would need to see
the body, to know how real it is how
the dad would not come back, so she
told him this is just the body, this is just
daddy's body, it looks so different
because it doesn't hold him anymore,
what we knew. Yes, yes, that's him
and then the boy crying and the mother
just touching the man's hair because
it is all that seems real. Someone takes
the boy away and she's just there with
the body, and after, just the boy.

David McCleery

My Mother Reading

To this day when I see a volume of
A Child's Christmas in Wales
it's 1967 and my Mother
is opening the book
and reading to me.

Candle, darkness, shadow, woods.
Even now I hear her words
and put the soft pillow of them to my ear.

She would read aloud
of poems with snow so deep
she had to lift her voice to walk home through it.

She would take me to the edge of the dark forest,
and suggest I wander off alone.
Oh, what a wild Mother to feed
such sweetness to a child so young.

I sat on one side, my sister on the other,
and together we learned to listen and be still.
We learned there was no shame in believing.

We loved beginnings and hated endings.
We wanted books to go on and on.

We loved what was beautiful and wicked,
the poor children that slept out on the ground,
the fierce old women,
and the small wren sitting in the window singing.

Are you listening?
She would ask.
I always was.

And once my sister fell asleep.

When she woke we reread page after page.
But I didn't mind.
It was a road I knew well.
The animals were still grazing in the fields,
the children came home again,
found the door open, the table set, the fire burning.

NANCY McCLEERY

Girl Talk (aristotle)

Told me so much I finally broke my silence,
told her when in the middle of life
you're an orphan, both parents dead,
with no lover, friends dying of love
and AIDS, when looking down and away
from some plateau to better see the seashore
or the shadow of yourself deep in some box canyon,
then what? The obvious so real it rarely gets said,
as Aristotle wrote? Aristotle who, after all,
abhorred the way music manipulates emotion,
and us remembering Mozart, putting in a CD—
his "Fantasia in C Minor."

      Told her forget
everything but making art, get to your studio,
new images. And focus, give yourself to paint again,
forget the men, your delicious melancholy
is eating you up, you need to feed it,
with color maybe.

       She answered: charcoal
and I'd like to go back to the door with that one
good man behind it. Then she shook her head.

I told her the older we get, the more complex.
Life, too? We can't redo the past?
We had the experience but somehow we missed
the meaning?

     Told me the two a.m. soul
goes solo sorry babe gotta run
my head's full of feathers at this hour.

And as abruptly as a darting sparrow, she left.
No parting shot, no words, only whistling.

Girl Talk (lists)

Now that she's back, I visited her in her studio
and she asked me whatcha' readin'? I showed her
the list of "Elegant Things" in Sei Shonagon's
Pillow Book come down to us from tenth-century Japan,
and she said,
                    I work from my own list
those things that look beautiful in sunlight

snow fallin' and tiny blue flowers on the rosemary
in my east kitchen window and shadows
of clouds floatin' on the river over fields
green winter wheat a rain storm
the single tear in my buddy Fred's left eye
just before he died of AIDS and
through a sunny window a meadow
of snow that no animal nobody not even me
had ever stepped into and

any of my sunlit paintings will fit in
with my impressionistic washes my visions
so what's on your list, she asked.

Told her maybe I'd write from her list!
And I add sounds and smells. Mourning doves
calling at dawn, the fragrance of mock orange
in bloom, ambulance sirens, soft wind
over wheat fields, spicy smells off the river,

and my mother coming out of the bathroom
laughing and saying it doesn't smell like roses
in there. And the jingle of my telephone, voices
of my adult son or daughter, my two
granddaughters or friends on the other end,
sun and moon eclipses, my two brothers.

She picked up her brushes. I walked
into the bright afternoon, humming.

Girl Talk (nine / 9)

Last time I saw her a few years back
before she went west to work the *saguaros,*
told me what goes around, goes around and around
and around and never seems to come around.
And she stopped talking about her love life,
the sad and occasional rolling down of a condom,
how perhaps her body had outlived its curiosity,
its instinct for pushing forward her sexual energy.
She stopped smoking, stopped stopping in
for girl talk and happily began taking prizes
for her drawings. And here I am, seeing
nine the unfinished number, wondering when or if
she'll drop me a card with her current address.

And me, tied to my barn, teaching, writing,
smoking, forgetting about rescues myself,
me skirting the rough edges of AIDS, thinking love
may be the last of the serious childhood diseases.

Though the night is warm and sensual,
the crescent moon showing her seductive smile
of promise, my bed remains empty. Fuck it, I say,
as she has. But finally, no: pencil and paper,
I say, for both of us; love, that temporary stay
against solitude; and art, too, the long reaches,
those arduous, amorous rides drawing us
toward and into whatever objects and subjects
the spirit/mind/heart, the body craves.

R. F. McEwen

John Davis

It was the three dogs came and then the boy
with bruises on his ankles where he'd run
against a thing that wouldn't move. But when
they saw John Davis wasn't dead they left.
Two dogs left first, and then the boy, and then
the other dog so that John Davis from
his back and with his knee cap grimacing
(or was it leering, lunging like an urge?)
called out between his teeth there must, by God,
be greater sport abroad than seeing him
destroyed. After thirty minutes, though, when it
was plain John's hurt went higher, deeper than
his knee, I wished the boy again so he
could run for someone larger than himself.
But just one dog returned much later on,
after John Davis died, and I was put
to leaving him to what the dog might do
while I was getting help to haul John home,
or keeping with John Davis through the night.
When light began to thin I shot the dog.

John Early Remembers the Moment of His Wife's Death

He remembered that he'd walked out toward the strand
late afternoon to fetch a net and found
his grandfather abroad with several more,
their faces snared in lashings of dark weeds
that crossed the caverns where their eyes would be
so that he had to catch his sleeve before
the old man caught the full of him and stepped
aside to kiss his cheek. Her sickness was
upon her five or seven days, but not
enough to hold him from the strand, or from
the sea itself, although those last two days
he'd kept to home and did what little bit
she might contrive until, late afternoon,
she'd had her cup, and he'd gone off to fetch the net.
Her glance upon him as he closed the gate
(he now imagined) would've coaxed him back

to say goodbye again. But when he met
his grandfather he knew that she was gone
because his grandfather was dead past forty years,
and all his boat were dead along with him
with not a one of them to find the shore.
On many nights to come John Early yearned
to resurrect that moment when he knew
his wife was dead, and feel the old man's lips
once more upon his cheek, unlearn his news.

J. J. McKenna

Face to Face

Inside the palm studded spa in San Lucas
the strong fingers of the masseuse apply
perfumes and warm oil like a country priest
offering extreme unction to a dying soul.
Outside the street waifs of Baja wait
patiently for the rich *norteamericanos*
who emerge from behind the iron gate
to squint and flinch in the bright foreign sun
as they step warily on their way
to the *mercado* to buy concha belts,
absurd sombreros, and bolo ties they will
never wear back home. In the dusty street,
the middle-aged tourists wear a clean new face
while the waifs, chafed by the harness of need,
put on that ancient, familiar face of those seeking alms.

JOHN MCKERNAN

I Chose the Gyroscope Because It Was Holy

& would never get lost in thorns & weeds
It was I think the last thing he ever

Loved on earth   I was stunned to silence
By his smile & his unrehearsed thank you
Though I bought it purely for myself

I gave up after my seventh year thinking
What on this earth I'd buy or steal
As a Christmas present for my father
Each thought making thought more impossible

In any way   The man had so few desires
A dry roof over our sleeping skulls
Food on the chipped plates   Clothes without
Patch or rip   Polished shoes without holes &
A patch of impossible grass in the front yard
I can still remember staring for an hour
Into the Woolworth's window on 16th Street
At the Wilson softball   Then at the gyroscope
Trying to imagine which would have more
Of him—Not me or us—in it & would stay
Still in balance while moving at full speed

I Would Trade Places With Your Death

Here   You can have this thin slice of light
Here you can lift your arms   Your hands

Again to curl them around that old ball bat
Cracked with splinters   Wrapped in black tape
The one that always smelled of potato salad

Some of the light will lie on the picnic table
Rusting its bright red color   The white plates
Waiting for their little squares of chocolate
Cake   The forks gooey with fudge frosting

110

Every object will be coated with sound
Of serious loud play   The old softball
Thumping into the flat catcher's mitt
The ping-chink of the bat pumping that ball
High to shortstop & a clean catch

You will come back if you can   Your white
Shirt glowing like the dawn   A baseball
Lifted high from the stinging wet weeds
Like a colossal day's sun in your hand
You will return as it floats though the air
Like a spinning host   You will arrive

Walking Along the Missouri River North Of Omaha I Find An Indian Arrowhead

The man who carried the first
Bible into Nebraska scoffed
At the grass ten feet tall

Called the blue sky a liar
Named the distance where nothing
& a further nothing beyond blooms

An evasion   This lack   This absence
The man with the book could not
Contend with   A land where

Man had never cursed life
Job is still hearing the first
Foot print on the west bank

Of the Missouri River   Year by year
Growing deafer dumber he hears
The whirr of the arrow

On its way to the heart of the deer

SARAH McKINSTRY-BROWN

Music Appreciation 101

My dad fell for my mother
because she looked like Joni Mitchell.
Nine shared rent checks and one pregnancy later,
my mom came home from the hospital to find him going ga ga
over the new Steely Dan album. I don't blame him;

a self made orphan, he cut down his family tree to build a bridge
from Kokomo to San Francisco that is still burning. And there's a reason

that before he taught me to ride a bike or throw
a left hook, my dad showed me how to hold a record
without touching its face; without leaving fingerprints,
scratches, evidence. My dad is proof

that ghosts exist. They come back for birthdays and Christmas.

From a distance he watched me grow into shoes, corsages, suitcases
and Greyhound buses. And there's a reason why a record reads
like a cross section of a fallen tree;
when my father pulls that album out of its cover,
a whole year of his life is right there
circling like kids on bikes in cul de sacs,
waiting for him to turn on the turntable,
place the needle on the groove,
and call them back home.

Sally Molini

Silk Shop on the Ganges

Varanasi

Chant drifts through the window
and I can see the swaddled bodies,
empty of what held them here.
Even at this distance I'd rather not watch
the blunt alchemy,
bone dissolved to flame,
earth uncurled, its tenuous states
of odor, ash and smoke
vanishing above the river
as Ranjit brings the scarves,
holds them up one by one,
each square half air,
half liquid prism.
Color cool to the touch,
just enough fabric for a wisp of dye.
I buy six. As he wraps them,
he tells how, after the *Bombyx mora*
spins its cocoon, the silk farmer
kills the chrysalis with a shot of steam
so its struggle to emerge
won't damage the precious thread.
He smiles, hands me the package,
promising the scarves will never bleed.

Charlene Neely

Unraveling

After the funeral
Grandmother sat
in her straight chair
methodically
unraveling Grandfather's
favorite sweater,
the pile of kinky, loose
thread growing at her feet.

Carefully undoing
each stitch she had knit
thirty years before,
not breaking the thread—
—not even once—
she let it drop
in its own pattern
and her pile grew.

She pulled the memories
one by one, telling
them as she went.
Recalling the days
and loves of her life
before laying them
at her feet—
a tale of yarn.

When the last stitch
was undone—the last
memory told,
without hesitation,
she knew the time was right
to pick up her needles
and re-knit her life
into a new form.

The needles clicked loudly
as she pulled the yarn
from its pile at her feet
and intertwined it
into a covering of love
for a baby who never knew
his grandfather but will be
protected by him, still.

ERNST NIEMANN

Refusal to Apologize for the Way Things Are

It was hardly necessary to identify the bodies.
Strange light struck the blue tile walls;
Promethian, perhaps, almost imaginary; troubling,
Thought one, like winter lightning, unexpected;
Exciting, thought another, the color of titian hair,
During the shelling off Malta, I felt like this,
Oddly horny couldn't get my boots on.

And the smells, too, were peculiar.
No, not patchouli, more like honeysuckle
To a child and nameless wildflowers,
Or burned black powder
On some far-flung 4th of July, or the more
Sophisticated cordite mingled with sea-rot—
A tightening between the eyes. A tendency
For the mind to wander—scenes of islands,
Cloudshapes, naked picnics in the hills,
Tempera paintings of peaceful kingdoms,
Whitewashed stone, even the crestfallen snow,
So many winter retreats: Stalingrad,
Constantinople, Ladysmith.

And was there music? Mumbled incantations?
Tinnitus? Or one sad, small angel
With a muted pennywhistle,
Breathless doodling, unlikely medium.
Sinuses popping open like Spring. The astounding
Ability to feel absolutely nothing—
Hallucinations, countless worlds,
Myriad Bodhisatvas passing in the West,
Unmade decisions, herukas.
And after all you've done for me,
Dropping like a pebble in a cold, deep well.

TERRANCE OBERST

Death and Company

well
I have been through all this
and it is not my fault
with my face
growing smaller and smaller in the mirror
and my eyes like red hornets
it is terrible
I was still a child
and now
with the wind raising
her dirty skirts
and my blood ticking time
to the north
I remember
that white house on Saylor Street
watching the dumptrucks
with my grandmother
who is dying in a rest home
O they are all dying
my friends
Tom Pate long and lanky
a sharp thud on a Canadian football helmet
Mike McCarthy
the rags of the priesthood
ground his slumping shoulders
Marilyn Morrow
face smashed against the dashboard
Tom Bisbee
decapitated on an icy night
in December
by a derailed train
and I sit in this dark apartment
and weep
testimonies of salt
for a lost shadow
in a roomful of shadows
until morning
climbs down from her apple tree
like a friendly child
to follow death
a face familiar in the crowd

Jan Pettit

Listening to the voices of poets long dead

Such old recordings, you cannot hear the words—
the movement of the voice is enough

like the rhythm of the hoe outside a window,
tonic of an auctioneer above a crowd. I watched

my grandmother write the poetry of quilts—
needle sink, needle rise. Cows coming in from tall grass

move like a dream, one behind another or together,
the slowest sheet waving. There is the trotting dog,

steady metal clank of bike chain, windmill, water pump.
On the playground, a long rope turns in the dust.

When you reach for me, I think of wind across a field
of brome, invisible hand musses the child's hair.

Haven't I been listening—since before bees swam
through alfalfa, flies circled the cow dung?

In a pasture in summer, grasshoppers are like punctuation.
I saw a woman with no arms—she smoked a cigarette

with her dirty feet. Bottles of milk rattle the same way
each time you open the icebox; screen door slams

with predictable audacity. Ring-around-the-rosy, twenty-third
psalm, announcer at the golf match, verse of concentration.

The piano with one ivory dead, high school bands in ragged formation.
My father always whistled the same seven notes, always off key.

Haven't I been listening since before you unfastened
the metronome, pushed me forward in the swing?

Kittens under the porch finally stop mewing, mewing,
mewing—the mother has returned from the hunt. Hopscotch,

pogo stick, four square, chainsaw in the distance
groans and bites, bites and groans.

The Waiting

maybe it was wrong to tell him he could go
if he wanted—I'd been there for days
or years, watching the bruises bloom
on his face, every place we touched
turned that color, like purple flowers
seeded from kisses. One nurse—Dorota,
could still find his eyes when no one could,
flirted shamelessly for that look of here—
so far past smiling by then. I had the drive
home and the children, secret mistrust
of time: So much waiting to be done—
waiting for the hands with the bedpan
and the rubber sheet, the gravied slabs of beef,
like theory of nourishment. Always,
new waiting replacing the old, forfeitures
the original self would never agree to:
walking, then standing, then breathing—
death wants so much. And even waiting
is not waiting, but a giving away of impatience,
dispersal sale of time, this moment
and the next and the next.

AMY PLETTNER

Meridians

In some Asian cultures there are names
for every nerve route, every tight meridian
squeezed between bone, muscle, and organ.

I think of the body
the mouth receives bread
the jaw knows rhythm
the tongue sends flavor to the mind.
Fingertips that hold onto the smell
of chopped garlic and onion,
carry the aroma all day into the rush of city.
How the skin remembers earth,
how the feet speak without interruption.

My friend's body smaller at eighty-six
twists to the left.
She no longer wants visitors or food.
She asks, *how long will it take?*
I know what she's asking.
A long time, I say.
What if I don't drink, then how long?
Longer than you think, and I think
of the Asian names involved in one body.
Returning current. Upright Branch. Fly and Scatter.
Crooked Marsh. Head Above Tears. Forward Valley.

Morning

Mom tells me to write about the largest
cottonwood in Platte County,
the one along Shell Creek's bank
in the middle of Saafeld's cornfield,
or write about Grammy's pink comb dipped into a glass of water.
But I'd rather write about my mother
in her blue robe
with the patio door slid open
to cool spring grass.
She smiles
looks over her shoulder at me,
"Do you hear them?"
And in comes song
filtered by thick cedar
a low soothed rhythm
of soft sand before waking,
The mourning dove's
coo-oo-oo coo coo
conversing down on my mother
making her face shine
as if her own mother's voice called
Alice Alice Marie Alice Marie.

Hilda Raz

Pets

The yard man is exactly the age of his dog,
six years, which is thirty-seven, he says
between lips chapped and swollen
from what he's been doing in the truck
with his helper. The dog waits,
the yard waits, filled with its pales
and spikes.
          The dog follows so closely
at his heels. Why?   He must be afraid
of being left behind, which must have happened
a time or two in the years he's been cherished.

What is a pet? Some thing
breathing, that's one. Some thing
warm, that's another. Something
to curl over when the world shuts
down for the night, or is it the body
shuts up, so tired, so ready
to exchange air freezing for
the warmth of...whatever is
in the bed, that pet we're discussing
as we fall down the lines here?

Pet, have you been cared for
long enough? Maybe not,
cold weeks alone in the nest,
a bucket by the bed, that whimper
from you as the others romp
and roll belly up for the scratch.

Whoever we are, surely we deserve
the moment each day when our eyes clear
to see that the loved face is ugly,
the hips turned inward, the fur patchy,
the eyes protuberant and blind,
the gait unsteady, don't we?
And that other one, who turns his back
on the scene? He always shows up again,
so we know he loves with keen hunger
and would adopt, take home, and set out for us
a bowl filled with every kind of kibble made
from tallow and the leftover flesh of our kind.

For Barbara, Who Brings a Green Stone in the Shape of a Triangle

From ocean
this porous shape
indisputably green
color I tell you
of healing, the color
I have chosen around me
like a vapor, this towel
on my shoulders, its green
drape an air over my scar,
then a shirt I pull over my head
and let fall for the green
lint-shed filaments of healing, moss
some ancestor might bind up with spit
and press onto my breast, no, the space
where my breast has been.
                              Yesterday
for the space of an hour, a woman
came here with her child, raised
up shirt, her breast was flesh.
The child pulled where her nipple
is, and touched his mouth
to her and filled himself.
She talked as he drank.
I listened to nipple,
a hiss of milk.
Miracle.

In your photos of green ocean
and boats, a line of women in green air,
their arms muscular, pulls against green water.
Their breasts are bare.
One, yours, shows a faint scar
my skin wears.

                    In the past year
I have given up four of the five organs
the body holds to call itself woman.
                    Green
Healer, today my body carries
in its clever hand the triangle
sea gave up to you
and you gave me.

                    I press it to my chest,
Empty of nipple, of milk, of nurture,
and feel you there: friend, lover
of women, teacher. You speak to me
each green vowel of the life language.

JIM REESE

Strike On the Stoop

When Vernon said to hell with it,
and decided not to stand in line
down at the corner
to see if he could get himself some work,
you knew it was going to be
one of those days.

Solly,
wearing his girlfriend's bikini briefs
and two different socks,
came out on the stoop
to see for himself.
Said, "If you ain't going, I ain't either."

Clarence,
who hasn't gone down
to the corner the last month and a half,
came out on the landing,
yawned, dug his hand in his shorts,
and scratched himself.

Then they sat. Watched
the bus go by,
watched kids go to and from school.
They saw the street sweeper
pass by twice, and called it
a day.

Ten Penny High

On Friday nights at Vernon's place
Felice, feeling loose,
unbuttoning clothes.

We chisel ice for our drinks
out of an old plastic ice-cream tub
long gone of vanilla and chocolate swirl.

The summer heat is unbearable.
Ice picks and iron fans,
humidity and cling.

Sitting on one of the kitchen's mismatched chairs
Felice spreads her legs wide
and starts icing her cleavage and lips.

Vernon plugs in the record player
and starts spinning forty-fives.
Felice grabs us, leads us in dance.

"I got songs to bring it up,
and songs to take it down," Vernon hollers.
"And don't be taking advantage of my wife, you hear?"

Before long Vernon drifts off
somewhere else, sometimes
physically, looking for what he calls his
ten penny high.

"Some sugar is right through
that bedroom door," Felice whispers,
tonguing our ears.

That's our cue to leave.
We all think about it on the way home.
Some of us talk about it,

some of us joke about it,
some of us, sitting in the back seat,
don't say a word.

Robert Ross

Tree

(after seeing Aske-win at the Sun Dance)

Suppose you are fifteen and beautiful
with a fine pair of dark upslanting eyes
but instead of living in a nice suburban house
and fighting with your mother over homework
and boys and TV and whether you cleaned your room
you live with your father when you can find him
(so busy with his drugs and with his women)
or with a 19-year-old lover
who practices the detached look of a criminal
and clings to you like your shadow
and who knows nothing useful—

You might dream a tree
that springs straight up from the ground
with roots that entwine your grandmothers
trunk silver as the moon
two bright uplifted branches
invoking the sky.
Each leaf would have a thousand shapes
each shape a thousand colors
each color would have the clear sweet voice
of fulfilled longing.

Because this is not possible
men go out in October
to walk the sodden earth.
Rotted by malice
woodpeckered by doubt
tunneled by itching colonies of lusts,
together they must choose a sound and living tree
that is wholesome and will serve their purposes.
In July when they chop it down
each chip will be wet with blood
and they will catch it on poles and in their arms
and carry it while women sing
and set it in the ground.
All will dance around the tree.
Some will tie themselves to it
by ropes pegged to their skin
and it will move to the rhythm of their heartbeat
until the thin skin breaks.

2.

Silent and not silent
the drums in your mind.
You drive back south to Texas
thinking of your westside students
how either they're idiots or you're an idiot,
or if no one is an idiot and you're one another's hope
then our culture has a sick transmission
and the country's tubed.
A physician flies home to Switzerland
to tend to her middle-aged patients,
mostly women who've been dumped by their husbands
and who've gotten tattoos.
Not a whit more sane than she is
one oar in the water
they're afraid of their lives.

3.

Much later, at the pith of the year
in the dead seething emptiness of Christmas
a man will leave off shrieking at his wife
and slam out into a blizzard
not caring whether he finds his way
not caring if he is found.

Marjorie Saiser

My Father Argued with my Mother

He said Why don't you want to talk about it?
and the straight line of her lips said
she had said all she was going to say,

and her flat back in her green sweater said
that was all he was going to hear from her.
He said he couldn't win.

I kept thinking somebody could win
but I couldn't find the starting line in that house.
All week I couldn't find the flags

or the silver trophy or the posted rules of the game.
I found my bedroom and I found my books
and a map with the names of rivers

on the crooked blue lines flowing east.
Child, go out the front door.
Find the wind; let it blow your hair across your face

because all night the wind
has been talking, promising *never again*
promising *always always*

and sometimes with little pieces of sleet
touching and touching
the smooth cool cheek of the window.

Night Flight

From 18F I see only the wing,
see only metal and rivets and painted black arrows
and partially worn off letters saying things like NO STEP.
From 18F, or anywhere on this plane,
I could see, if I want to, the video.
I could, evidently, watch ads for Buzz Lightyear, the series.
But I am watching *us,* the community
of 1090 to Denver. We are facing forward
as though in a tunnel or tube,

dots of light in a row above our heads.
We are ranks of readers, sleepers,

or we are the cast of *Our Town;*
We are cast as the dear departed,
sitting on stage on our chairs—supposed to be graves—
looking straight ahead, talking among ourselves,
never looking at Emily the living,
when she comes to visit the cemetery.
We are not turning toward Emily;

we are numbers and letters facing forward.
From 18F I see we are regular in our posture,
regular in our habits.

In my row we are raising similar cups from similar trays,
oddly comforting:
now this head, now that one, lowers to drink.
One by one we sip our mutual nectar;
one by one we set it down.

Paradise on the Niobrara

The beef and potatoes on her plate
matched the beef and potatoes on mine.
Her hands and face the family dog licked,
same as mine. Someone brushed her hair, brushed mine.
Blizzard after blizzard we shrugged into dark coats and ratty boots
and walked into the tedious cold.

Same this, same that, she tells me today,
but every thing different just the same.
You call that loving, she says,
that was crazy-making, that was crap.
You were always looking at the skyline,
singing with the chorus.
I had a solo.
I flew in close to the hipbones of the buildings,
my stomach empty,
my fists like rocks.

Mark Sanders

Custody

The man drove slowly away from his children,
watching them in his rearview mirror.
The daughter, tall for her age, waved and waved and waved.
And the man had hoped to see her frown,
as if the wave of the arm, the hand,
were a wiper on a windshield, slapping off the sky's grief.
But everything was in reverse—
she seemed to smile, to be happier than he wanted.
But the mirror distorts like a mind does.

The older son made his way up the stairs
that led to his mother's apartment. He had not looked back.
What could this mean? The stairs
should have been impossible—a mountain, craggy
and slippery. He should have been there
at the mountain's bottom to catch the boy.
But, he kept climbing, looking upward,
making his way to the cave of himself.

The younger boy leapt off the bottom step
and, the man thought, went running toward the car.
The man saw his mouth was open.
He heard, beyond the engine's noise
and the doo-da of the radio, his son's voice
calling him back. *Stop, Daddy, stop,*
that voice called. It was the voice the small one
had used when his father had come into his room
to scare the ghosts away so that he could sleep.

How long ago had that been? Years, already.
The man stopped, put the car into reverse,
and backed. *What is it?* the man asked.
The son, perplexed, explained he was only running
to the neighbor's house to play.
It was well, then. Well. Well—then.

The man drove to the exit of the apartment complex,
past wrought iron gates suspended
from brick pedestals. A wicked turn left,
a knoll, and, as way leads to way,
the knoll lifted him up, let him down,
and the complex disappeared.

Talking November Weather, Long Distance

Again, across the miles, my mother's voice
is optic thin. Are you sick, I ask. The weather,
she says, so hot one day, cold the next.
The wind will not stop blowing, and there's dust
and mold in the air. It's not just her,
she tells, but my sister and nephews have it, too,
getting over it, getting it back.
Isn't that the way the weather works,
moving from one extreme to the other?
I used to think it was so, but where I live
Texas heat is perpetual. My body rains.

We talk about my oldest sister's family,
the woman, who, angry at her cancer,
connected it to my divorce and refused to death to speak.
Have you heard from any of them, I question.
No, no, nothing. It's hard for them,
now Dee is gone. But, I remind her,
it was hard when Dee was here, for everyone.
Yes, yes, that's true. The weatherman says
the snow will fall deep. I may have to shovel.
Can't you find someone to do that for you?
I know I'm wasting air. She's 75,
her body like a piece of lattice.
Mom, if you fall, it will be hard to get back up.
O, we all get back up until it's time not to.
Then someone else can breathe the dust
we used to breathe, shovel the snow
we no longer feel the weight of.

Death's Door

Finding yourself at Death's door
is like driving through a pleasant countryside,
all hills and valleys, the pitch of steep,
the pit of river, the end of vacation.
It's the piddling up and down the elm-lined streets
of a small town, the middle-class panorama.
Green lawns and pregnant trashcans at the curbs
awaiting delivery. We never know which house
is Death's, exactly, nor which driveway
will lure us in. We never know, until, like epiphany,
the door we can't resist appears,
and it's a short walk up a stone path,
flower plots filled with lilies of the valley and jonquils;
a blue spruce looming above the front stoop,
needles red and brown like a carpet
where the grass should grow were there sun,
were there more than the gray dust that drought
has laid there. The porch wears recent paint,
but beneath the new enamel old regrets flake
or bear the scars of someone
who tried to scrape them smooth.
A porch swing but Death doesn't swing.
Wicker furniture for hot summer days,
a glass of tea or red wine,
but Death stays cool inside the house, in shadows,
awaiting the visitor who comes to poke
the doorbell with painful inquisition.
Were it not for the busybodies, Death would read
last words from whatever lost books
he found on his shelves. He would eat
whatever last supper fit his plate.
He would nap and prepare.
The visitors all want to see what he's done with the house.
Come on in, Death says, *let me make you feel at home.*

Roy Scheele

At the North Edge of Town

It is one of those stories hidden away
in the local histories, out of sight
of all but those-who-stumble-upon, and when
you come to it at last, whether by
accident or the sheer luck of not looking,
it is like kicking at leaves and releasing
a small spring at your feet—the book falls
open to the place, you take one look
and it wavers.

Then leaf by leaf you peel away
what time has done, and it all
comes clear again, peaceable, still: how
once, somewhere near here, a man took
his living out of the streams, setting out
trotlines I like to think of as willow,
that would bend down to the water
and not break, holding in tow for him, when he
came to haul them in, the bounty
of this deep land—catfish, carp and
buffalo—to sell for what they might bring.
He lived in a shack by a lost landmark
and knew a good thing.

        Now I see him
come up again at evening from the creek,
his glance lighting far back in the branches,
weaving the sunlight into a look he wears
at the corners of his eyes looking past me
into this future of garbage waters, the veins
of his life gone hard at the edge of factories,
junked cars turning even the earth dirty,
and I fold that look back into the leaves
of the book, stopping his mouth with them,
his innocent questioning.

TERRY LEE SCHIFFERNS

When They Go

My dog, Thelma, taught her pup
how to sit for biscuits and chew on sticks
and bark at coyotes in the distance
and chase cars that came down our lane.

Today, Thelma sits on the ridge next to the windmill
looking out toward the river as if on guard or watch
just a couple of feet from where I buried
her half grown pup last week, and I wonder
if dogs feel remorse or regret.

Inside, my oldest son has picked my cupboards clean.
The green tea I bought at the specialty store—
gone. And this morning, I couldn't find a washcloth
to save my life. Like the toothpaste and shampoo,
pens, and that part of my life I'll never get back,
they have gone away to college.

And what I should have and shouldn't have said
on my son's first night home when he drank and drove
through the neighbor's fence plays over and over again
in my head. But what can a mother know?

I dug the hole deep, knowing if I didn't
Thelma would dig her daughter up and I'd have to bury
her again. I call Thelma from her lookout to come inside
where I will give her a biscuit and we will go on.

Barbara Schmitz

How to Get to Plattsmouth

It's there. Smack dab in the Midwest.
Where the Platte and the Missouri
meet and kiss and keep on moving,
chugging to the Mississippi.

It's high on hills that are hard
to climb in winter. Ice covered.
Cars and shoes sliding backward.

Oak and acorn covered.

Older than Omaha. An old
river town.

President Truman stood on
the balcony of a caboose
there: stopped for
a couple minutes. After
the war was over.

The flood waters would raise
their hips in spring. Daring
to sashay to the end of Main
Street. Almost all the way
up to the meat lockers once.

More bars per capita than
any other little town in
the 40's

Lots of hot rods zooming
around the A & W Rootbeer stand.

The high school was on top
of the hill with funny old
teachers: Margaret Kruse
who taught geometry *and*
English, Kleenex stuffed
in her low cut dress, spraying
saliva on the students in the
front row. Cecil Comstock,
hand, palm up, on his shoulder, reciting.
Joyce Kilmer's "Trees." The Coach we

called "Possum" and painted swastikas
on his history room door.

South of Offutt Air Force Base,
Strategic Air Command, Ground
Zero in the 50's. A special
command center underground
where the war would be fought
in case of nuclear attack.

Safe enough for a young girl
to walk home at night after
a ball game, a dance...(my
father said if anyone grabbed
me, they'd let me go at
the first street light.)

It's still there. 20 miles
South of Omaha, around Dead
Man's Curve, past what used to be
Merritt's Beach. You can come
in on the highway next to the cemetery,
where my great grandparents, Czech
grandparents, uncle and aunts, mother
and father, one cousin my age
remain—silent lookouts, cherishing
Plattsmouth's fragments in their
crumbling, letting go bones.

Supper

I'm making a tuna casserole,
adding white and green noodles
to water boiling in a cast iron pan.
He's fixing the broken boards
in the fence. Our son's off playing.

I resist the urge to go to the back door,
storm glass still on,
and wave a movie wave
across the green grass, across
the theater, across eternity.

All the couples "forever
and ever, Amen" repeating

this scene, wearing these costumes
complete with opposite sets of genitals
as if they were real, and we existed,
he and I, in this time,
this old house, supper almost ready.

KAREN GETTERT SHOEMAKER

Learning To Love My Belly

My bare feet float above my pelvis,
which is propped up on a rectangular block.
A strap wraps my shoulders down my back.

I am strangely comfortable here
on the basement floor of this church
in a row of women like me, our changes

full and soft upon us. When Rita tells us
to listen to our bodies, I try to focus

on my breath, moving it, as Rita tells me to do,
like a bicycle chain: inhale up the front of my body,
exhale down the back, and in up the front again.

My bare feet above me are my dead father's feet.
Bones and sinew stringing from ankle to toe,
coarse nails in want of care.

His long fingered hands rest on my belly,
rising softly with each chaining of my breath.

Michael Skau

Winter at Ram's Horn Mountain

The pine and aspen branches scarcely hold
the weight of the snow as it sits like a drunk on a stool
in a bar, leaning this way and that, ever
on the brink of losing control, tilting over,
falling down. But winter, always watchful,
sobers the snow with tension of the cold.

Deer scat on the ground, perfect little pellets,
squats sunk like a campfire burnt to sullen coals.
Animal tracks dart through the trees and scrub
and radiate out in spokes from a frigid hub,
anxious to evade the threat from occasional
cartridges: shotgun shells and spent bullets.

Language too has its dangers at this height.
A spoken word can cause the snow to fall:
disturbing the trees and forcing limbs to cease
their rigid pose, the sound betrays the peace
twice—suspended snow, from above in a bundle,
with a smothered gasp, plummets down out of sight.

JAMES SOLHEIM

Blessed by Meteors and by the Benevolent Men of Space

I woke. Left my bed. Stood right here,
where I've marked the spot for grandchildren.
Toes snug in carpet, I saw the kitchen flare
with wavering light. Saw the colander—
humped up to dry—saw the noteboard—could almost
read my notes. All from the light of a meteor
lodged in the floor. To have your roof
struck once makes a house—and you—seem small.
Struck twice, you're blessed. See that hole—
the facsimile I made?—put one hand on it.
Feel the hot and cold drive to the bone.
It almost gives me the vertigo again. Once a month
or so ships come—with light that's not
quite light, a drone...They land softly in the grove.
They leave as gifts the usual—alloys
not possible on earth, some dirt from Mars.
I've seen them lolling above the church—
each time I pass I touch the graves, and get
a tingling in my hand. It almost hurts.
Here's a model of their ship, a diorama
of the time they stole the laundry off my line.
Here's a photo—bad, I'll admit—
of their light as seen from behind the shed.
I learned from them the dizziness
inside the tree, the rendezvous
of cell to cell in the guts of birds,
the ache within the crystal—a kind of life.
This replica's of the flag they set
outside the ship before they hypnotized the dogs
I lost—three purebreds, collies—and a goat.
I sleep now in the woods, among the fairy rings
their landing leaves. There must be ten.
You ought to sleep out there with me tonight.
With what it does to you—the light, the spinning—
you can spend a year in fourteen days. Feel
the murmur of their radios. Feel the waves
of static from their eyes, They're
listening. This all will be utopia soon.

Judith Sornberger

Our Lady of the Rest Stop

Last time I saw her—no kidding—
she was descending from a beat-up
Winnebago in the Sandhills just north
of Hyannis, Nebraska, wearing blue,
like always, except now
it's a wind-bleached denim sundress.

And this time there's no halo
except around everything
in her vicinity: the kids pulling fish
from the river, the fish themselves—
their fins like pearly wings—
the vials of wild plum wine
someone has left in the shallows,
cooling. The cooing pair
of doves pecking at pebbles.

And when she shakes your hand
it too starts glowing, not
so you can see it, but so you know
finally how good it is
to have a palm and fingers.
And all you want to do is
spread that sheen on everything
you can get your hands on,

to make it feel
like it's just been washed
in brightest water
as though it is a fish
that dreamed itself
into an angel.

Wallpapering to Patsy Cline

for my mother and sister

We're here to cover the cracks
in the wall, to forgive the bad
taste of previous owners, to bury
the orange and brown daisies in a service
transforming this home into yours, sister.
We don't drywall or drive nails,
but like our mother's mother, a good seamstress,
we know how to make an offcast
garment fit our wishes. We form
a procession we've practiced before,
kitchen to dining room, this time bearing
drop cloths, utensils, dutch ovens of paste.

Patsy sings us through some stripping:

>   *I*
>
>   *fall*
>
> *to*
>
>   *piec-*
>
>   *es...*

a tune we know too well. We work
as when my ballerinas, your floral stripes,
and Mom's teacup scenes met in the hallway's
neutral eggshell. There are too many generations
of wallpaper here to strip. We stop
when we come to fully petalled cabbage roses.

Patsy says she has to choose today
between a poor man's roses
and a rich man's gold.
Choose the gold, we're yelling,
giddy in the futility of warning.
We're brushing bubbles to the bottom, giggling,
but they won't be brushed away,
and we find they're buried
under the old paper, an error made
so far back we can't hope to mend it.
Choose the gold, Patsy,
and buy yourself some roses.

And now she loves him

so-o-o-o

           much

    it hurts her,

a sob in her voice we recognize,
having heard it often in each other's.
But Mother, Sister, *deep within my heart
lies a melody,* one that doesn't twang
with regret. Patsy's right,
we need some loving too.
Yes, we do.
Indeed we do.
You know we do.

But look at the room we've created:
pastels of triangles, lovers' triangles—
but not in that old, stripped-down usage.
Think of them as pyramids, homes to hold us
forever, a woman at each angle.

MARY K. STILLWELL

The Circle Dance

The great circle dance at the September powwow
is about to begin but
this family has lost a child
over the summer and the grief must be combed
from their hair before they can enter
the circle. The mother walks the grasses
to the west side of the circle. The father
walks the grasses, then the other children,
then the aunts and uncles of this family
who has lost one of its children to accident
over the summer. They stand just outside
the circle, and the old people come with

finger combs and begin running them through
the hair of the family, combing the grief
from the mother, the father, each sister and brother,
aunts and uncles, combing out the grief
like snarls, casting out grief
in tangles. On the north side of the circle,
my scalp tingles. It is grief caught
in my own hair, and I must comb it out
if I am to join the circle. I, too, use my fingers
as a comb, pushing the hair up from the head
and away so the grief can loosen.
This combing takes some time,

and the family begins to cry and the old people,
too, begin to cry, and I on my side of the circle
begin to cry. Tears and grief spill
over my shoulders and run down my legs.
Tears and grief spill over their shoulders
and run down their legs.
The earth receives it as rain, takes it in
as if it were her own because it is her own.
From it she has already begun to fashion
new children to send to us. We
bow to the wisdom of the old people,
enter the circle that we may dance.

Red Barn

"See the pegs there," I said and pointed,
and the insurance inspector looked;
I can't remember what he said,
but the wide side door of the barn had been rolled open
and I could see two pegs holding a beam in place.

The red barn color is a particular red.
My stepfather worked steadily every day
of his life there keeping up the buildings:
barn and corn crib, milk and cob houses,
cattle shed and chicken coops, the lean-to.

Later he poured concrete where the manger had been,
where I milked Roanie and later Chocolate before school,
because he thought there was money in hogs.
I hear cows stomp for flies, pigs squeal,
and this silence. "If you want to insure the barn,"
he says, "you'll have to nail over with corrugated tin."

I look up, past the loft tight with bales,
with the warm sweet smell of living things all around
and the kitten the barn cat finally had, the one that survived,
and the feeding-bin full of oats where the chute
was already worn smooth by the time I moved here,
to where the owl sat every night like a stone column
his head cocked for field mice.
And over there's where we rang the hogs
and put the heifers for shelter starting January.

The two plots of land side by side have passed
to my brother and me, and we each live
our own 100 miles away and rarely see each other.
It's the land that keeps us in touch, and, if we don't sell,
that we will pass to our four children
who will remember their grandmother as an old woman.
They will half remember the stories we force on them
and only then after we are dead and they have buried us.

There is not corrugated tin enough to protect anything
from weathering, no insurance with life benefits.
The windows look to the east to let in light
for the sows when they lay farrowing,
overlook the road that took me elsewhere,
and brought me back home again.

Therese Svoboda

Sale Barn

All the cows with bar code
on their backs get run through,
the wind like a big pneumonia
across all that hide, then
all the reds sell high.

The sold song of a two-way radio—
you hear that cut by the fence,
ears that cold. Well, impossible-to-repress
this fever of selling. Well, nigh impossible,
the free puppies go free.

How do we total up?
The inarticulate gesticulate—
it's not hard, it's as hard as
ice in shade. One finger up,
then trucks, the butcher.

Kim Tedrow

Recent Angels

For Tina Geraci

If you see her you will know her
By the way she glances sideways
As you pass. Keeps you at
the edge of her sight. She is one

who knows silence as native language,
and fog as cloud fallen to earth
to slow recent angels in their
haste to rise. It is the breath

of those who die young, who are
alone late, and it is your silence,
by which she knows you.
She has heard this silence before.
It is her name, not spoken,
Over and over and over again.

Ruth Thone

December 1

A Liturgical Year

If you think you will get
your life back, your old
regular life, you won't.
It's been two years now and
my nightly face cream still
sits unused on the sink shelf,
the five meditation books
occasionally opened to no avail.
Just now I have encountered
another level of grief, irrational
anger and deep sadness, finally
to recognize I shall live out
my life
brain-injured.
We're all doing time. Maybe I
can find freedom in being
a monk in here, sitting still
for ten minutes a day, reflecting
on my life,
watching two blue jays hop
under the bird feeders
splendid against the cold dead grass.

Jon Volkmer

Cosmology

Adam, still a child of God,
naked and alone,
was brought each new-made creature,
from air and land and foam.

Whatever name he gave to them
that the name would be:
You are ox and elephant,
And you, my friend, are flea.

What an angry jealous God
He turned out to be.
It's nice to recall when he acted
kindly, playfully.

And when my father made the bins,
he didn't often smile,
but gave my brother Ron a brush
and let him loose awhile.

Years later it became my turn
To work around the mill,
And find the names my brother left
were on the grain bins still.

CORN BALL stood by TALL CORN
and KING LEONARDO.
MEINKEL (named for brother Mike),
LEFTY and LITTLE MOE.

The star of Hitchcock's *Vertigo*
got a bin named BEAUTIFUL KIM.
BIG BAD JOHN came from a song
at my brother's whim.

No one ever could have guessed
how they comforted me,
amid the sweat and heat and dust,
this stalwart company.

So here's to Adam and to Ron,
and life before the fall,
gentle fathers, newborn names,
ESQUIRE and BABY DOLL.

Fumigant

I drag the cans across mountains of grain,
carpeted inches thick with grasshoppers
and assorted furious winged things

swarming into my teeth, nose, eyes,
blurring the half-light beneath the hot
steel roof. Without a Pharaoh to impress

I am left with merely scientific means
of deliverance, as I crab across a reddish sea
of dirty sorghum and bug debris.

Screwdriver my rod and staff, I jam holes
to make it a sprinkler can, and anoint the piles
all the way back to the ceiling hatch.

My father must have seen me stagger down,
blink in uncertain sunlight, headache
drenched, reeking petrochemical stench.

I am still afraid, decades away,
of toxins waiting to unfurl their flag
and claim my irredentist lungs.

But each time I start to call him to account,
I recall the tons of dust he ate,
the runaway boxcars, falls from ladders,

power tool slips, the miles of frayed
electrical wires, and inhaling the mistakes
of anhydrous ammonia and propane tanks.

I picture him, so cranky and alive
at eighty-five, and think too of his wife,
baking bread in a sturdy house, and dead

at fifty-three. Where was I, the Whirlwind
asks, when earth's foundations were laid?
Where was I when the morning stars sang?

SARAH VOSS

Holy, Holy, Holy

this day when Coalition forces finally kill
a long-sought enemy in the Middle East,
when the President arrives/departs our city
with no unseemly incident, leaves behind
relieved lawmen, limp observations
about immigrants, border control, America,
when the perpetrators of four separate
but ghastly murders this year remain free
and yesterday's news, and the morning paper
front-pages a downtown tax, school districts
which continue to sport Indian mascots,
causing state educators consternation

this day when one woman, a thousand miles
east, heads for work wondering how much
longer her cancer-ridden husband will last, when
Mr. & Mrs. Long-Married check airline schedules
so they can fly a thousand miles west to visit
their grown son living (barely) with congestive
heart disease, when two people who don't
even know each other, take the same anti-
depressants prescribed by the same doctor,
and John Doe (sober, suicidal, celebrating
his 61st birthday) wonders if he can make it
another year until social security kicks in

this day when the geranium cuts wintered
indoors are rooting, budding in the back yard,
when the old neighbor man, repairs complete,
wheels a small bicycle down the street
for the little neighbor girl to ride, when, two states
away, the four grandchildren climb into car seats
(the law requiring ever more precautions)
and my daughter loads a picnic in the back,
drives to the pool, when I, just off the phone
with her, trim the roses my spouse gave me after
Monday's surgery, check my newly-biopsied
breast, note the bleeding has actually stopped

Have You Reached the Part About the Lightning?

With appreciation to Michael Gruber
for his *Valley of Bones*

He asks, then asks again, sure I'll like it. Eager,
I turn pages, days. My faith, a devoted dog.

Suffering, dope lords, cop and psychologist
in love. Doubters, murders, fears. The black
Cuban and his mother whom everyone liked.

I read in snatches:
cat on my lap
with mocha at the bookstore
visiting the grandkids
couched in my library my back hurting again.

Words bathe me. I luxuriate in their bubbles,
keep turning. Maybe the lightening
will be next, tomorrow. Lightning.
Lightening lightning.

The pages burst with conundrums:
God and belief
the Shiny One and Christians
gold Twinkies thrown down from heaven
both bad and good.

From what he said, I won't find
the part about the lightning until
maybe the middle

but I pass the halfway mark one noon waiting
in the Jeep for him to finish an errand at Lowes.

Old now, I read like a beggar yet still no
lightning. But the snow blowing tonight,
(a blizzard advisory) is another thing altogether

and us snug inside,
raiding the refrigerator for leftover turkey,
satisfied.

LYNN OVERHOLT WAKE

Middle Creek

Look south
just after you pass
the road to Garland

fourteen ponies
pastured
in the sun

of course, the ponies
are not always
waiting

and on those days
I make do

but today
February 29
I believe someone

has arranged them
notes
on a golden hillside
sacred music

Understory

Lilies and peonies and babies' breath
all got along together the summer I moved in.

Now they're way too chummy. Probably should dig them up,
dig up something, anyway, maybe that whole perennial bed.

Guess I need to redesign the garden I bought into,
but that's not really what I want.

What I want
is for this world beginning at my kitchen door

to be what it wants to be
as it shimmers and beckons and sings

this first Friday in October—
too early to rake the bubbled hackberry leaves,

dry messages gathering in the corners of the patio
like shy guests at a party finding each other.

The pin oak flashes gold on her left hand,
While our neighbor's amur maple blushes red.

I want to say to twelve-year-old girls

don't worry, just be yourself.
I want that to be true.

Rex Walton

When She Does Not Come Home

My daughter calls, from her cellphone,
in the cold, on the corner down from
her house on 50th: the cat is gone.

Why, she says, do I worry about this
old white thing, when every time she
comes back with no apologies after
days missing?   I don't answer.

She goes on, counting the times around
the block, on foot, calling in the dusk
of January, the snow changing from sun-lit
to snow-lit, a byproduct of the dim yellow
streetlamp, and the red-gray sky. It is cold.

Even over the phone it is cold. The snow
stops melting. The dirty ice on the inter-
section is quiet, recombining what water
is left—bringing it back into itself, shifting
the earth three notches forward in the process.

Even here, at home, the thermostat whispering
heat to the furnace, the bulbs quietly converting
electrons to light, I shift inside myself, finding
that dirty little white cat in my sights, too—now
I see her in the dried, barren lilac bush at the end

of the parkway, now frozen in headlamps, car horns,
in the third lane of North 48th Street, her eyes
widen, yellow-gleaming a smaller mix of the color
of streetlamp and ancient dreams. The snow there
tire-tracked, transitory, salt-laden, gleaming—

a Mid-Eastern Dead Sea caught in the fractured
avenue, the shoreline caught with snow villages
perched on both curbstones. I blink, and shiver
in my 70 degrees and good lighting, standing
on the landing, halfway to the second floor. I see

somewhere a path opening, the cat coming home
in its own good and proper time. Somehow, I will
find a way to tell this to my daughter, jazzed-out
and jittery on the corner across from the street sign,
the street lamp, the darkening trees. She doe not

know it yet, but days down the road, the cat comes
home. My daughter tells me, over and over, the cat
is gone, not yet seeing days away, the screendoor
glass showing her dirty snowball of a feline, grimy
and nonchalant on the porchrail, waiting to be let in,

to sidle by, toward the foodbowl, the waterdish,
the indentation on the back of the couch, without
one glance of explanation or apology, without even
an air of guilt. My daughter does not yet feel the door
open under her hand, as the cat comes in, yet already

preparing for the next leaving, the next final good-bye.
I don't say anything. I imagine my daughter, instead,
now seeing her daughter gone, years from now, gone
that first time overnight without a call, without a note,
without a word of warning. I remember when I held

my breath for days, when my daughter roamed the night
streets, for night after night, only to slip in at 3 a.m.,
through the basement window, then come upstairs
in the morning, as if nothing unusual happened in the
course of the planets that day. I would come down

the hall, hearing a noise, find her sitting at the kitchen
table, calmly eating a bowl of Cheerios. And drinking
a glass of milk. I would say to her, well, what would
I say to her, after all these mornings like this, finding her
alive and crunching cereal, staring at the morning news?

COREEN WEES

On the Death of Lura Walcott,
Wife of the Famous Paleontologist

Last night she awoke, 3 a.m.,
coughing up the tiny ones,

Agnostus pisiformis, trilobites,
bits of stone hitting her teeth

as they flew from her mouth
until the bed was filled—

heavy and gray as the Burgess Shale.
Then, in the thickening dust, they

gathered, the great paleontologists,
her husband, Charles, among them,

the wisps of their brushes over her body
soon lulling her back to sleep.

Next time she awoke, near dawn,
Charles was kneeling over her

prying a curled specimen,
Ceraurus pleurexanthemus,

from her chest, from the region near
the heart. In normal circumstances

the legs would have rotted
quickly, but this specimen

has been carefully preserved,
so he is hopeful. He will spend

months slicing it thin as lunchmeat,
polishing each section, searching

for the most elusive of fossils,
trilobite limbs, traces

of soft parts he hopes might
somehow have been spared.

DON WELCH

Funeral at Ansley

I write of a cemetery,
of the perpetual care of buffalo grass,
of kingbirds and catbirds
and cottonwoods;

of wild roses around headstones,
with their high thin stems
and their tight tines
and their blooms pursed
in the morning.

I write of old faces,
of cotton hose and flowered dresses
and mouths which have grown up
on the weather.

And I write of one woman
who lies a last time in the long sun
of August, uncramped by the wind
which autumns each one of us

under catbirds and kingbirds
and cottonwoods, and the gray-green
leaves of the buffalo grass.

Nebraska

Going west when the sun is going down,
following the highways like light cords.

•

If Nebraska were the name of a Russian woman,
they could love her.

There would be a certain large-boned beauty about her.

Or she would be dressed in black and lace.
Her waist would be small,

and she would drag her long dress over a floor
into a study lined with French books.

She would be a pawn in huge novels of war.

.

As it is, she is a woman of spare beauty.

.

Turning away from him so that the fine hollows
of her back were toward the bed,
she said, Why do you do this to me?

Why do you keep imagining me in other places
and states?

And why do you keep assuming our children
are unhappy?

The Keeper of Miniature Deer

The keeper of miniature deer
was an old man with stiff knees.
He had the straight eyes of a child,
and he walked the emperor's grounds
speaking to the white swans
and the empress's pheasants.
In the compound of red deer,
among the musk and estrus,
he was especially fond of two old ones
born joined at the shoulders,
a stag with its rack huge and carbuncular
spreading out over a doe,
the old doe with eyes like fitful oil
over water. And he who knew nothing
of life after death, who lived
only to serve the miniature deer,
let them eat from his hands,
holding out salt in one,
in the other, grain,
softly calling their names,
saying, *Mother* and *Father.*

KATHLEENE WEST

Progression

You are the farmer's daughter,
corn-fed, apple-cheeked,
a local yokel from a jerkwater town
where tractors cruise the gut on Main Street
and Loretta keeps tabs from the five and dime.

You are the round little Swede,
snub-nosed, tongue-tied,
who rises at the crack of dawn
to milk the cows, slop the hogs
and cut across the corn to school.

You are the first to go to college
one hundred homesick miles away,
straw behind ear, manure on shoes,
and a coke date after the Kansas game
where Husky the Corncob yelled in your face.

You marry the hayseed in ROTC blue,
decide graduate school's not for you,
pack Sunbeam skillet and Bake-King tin
to honeymoon at the Holiday Inn
where Tom and Sharon put cornflakes in the bed
and undutiful thoughts come into your head.
You are not the first to divorce:
"Grandma did and *she* was good!"
but Grandmother left that city slicker,
let him go straight to the dogs with corn liquor
and settled down with an old-country man.

Your lovers are men who never remember
if you're Iowa-born or Dakota-bred
but they've all hit I-80 on the way to Frisco,
sent corny postcards from Bosselman's Café:
"God, but I miss you. God, but it's flat."

You are the ugly American
in blue jeans, t-shirts and mirror shades.
The dollar's strong, your accent's stronger,
cracking gum, munching popcorn, peanut butter, chocolate bars—
"Why *can't* the Europeans take us like we are?"

You are home again, home again, wiser of course.
"Fine," you practice, like a salesman's spiel.
The same old cornfield east of the house,
Mom and Dad on the stoop, with the usual joke,
"Always glad to see you come—always glad to see you go."

JAN CHISM WRIGHT

September 11th

A woodpecker hammers
for his daily dinner.
The horned owls in the bog
have again begun to hoot.
The crickets chirp with
the self-same insistence.
The corn stands, still,
still ready for harvest.
It occurs to me how easily
this earth could do without us.

David Wyatt

Enough Driving

Tonight I find a good room in the Super 8,
pictures everywhere, of horses, ragged mountains,
slight snow. I empty my pockets,
knowing the wind is painted with traces of pink.

I look at my eyes, unlit lamps, in the mirror. The ceiling
pounds out the arrival of unknown beasts.
I never feel quite myself in a room like this,
despite the solitude, the t.v. watching.

At no time am I afraid of death, though I think to
be found here right after sunrise by a housekeeper
who speaks no English—"este muerto"—
would increase my chances of being talked about later.

I manage, still awake, to hear the surf
in the painting above the bed, while over by the window
the heater, suddenly alive, plays with the thick
maroon curtain like some guy who has put his hand
under his girlfriend's skirt.

Out of politeness,
I turn away.

Man With Green Thumb

You want to plant a garden
but you don't take the time,
your neighbor, who works as hard
as you, every day up at dawn
to get to a job that lasts
till nighfall—your neighbor
has a huge garden, of cannas
and of corn, black-eyed susans
dominate a section, tomatoes,
yarrow, coneflowers; he
has placed stones around
impatiens and built raised beds
of bleeding hearts with other
stones. He works at midnight,
he must, or when the stars have been out
so long they too should be tired. You
never see him in daylight
with a hoe or a watering can,
with seed or fertilizer, his wife,
often inside, occasionally
waters a hanging plant
on the porch—she's pregnant again.
How does he do it? The children
playing a good distance
from the garden. When does
he have a chance to teach such
reverence? Your own sons
treat hostas like dirt and run
through the few petunias
near the front door until
the flowers' faces are dust, your wife
once a rose in your eyes,
has been gone for months. You sleep
without fulfillment, lie awake
hearing nothing of your
neighbor's efforts and yet new
blossoms are there every morning,
even under clouds or after days
of no rain. What is his secret?
You live so close to it,
the same birds fly
between his place
and your dry Pampas grasses,
beneath which your cat
takes shelter in the midday heat.

Rosemary Zumpfe

Remembrance

What is the color of remembrance?
What shapes a glove when I slip it from my hand?

•

In my closet—old moccasins slumped under a gold Hindi dress,
Grandmother's Czekoslovenske´ vysívaní folded on the shelf,
statue of a Ghana queen, green frog beaded on her forehead,
Kwan-Yin carved from a stump of bloodwood,
curled oak leaf stained alizarin by the sun.

•

Blood running hungry to Ellis Island. Bronze woman,
I won't dream my mother's girlhood dream
suffused in the sweet bruised fumes
of crates of bananas handed out at your feet.

•

Refugee. Expatriate. Exile. Emigre´.
Let us bow our heads.
Weep for the roses that have lost their petals.

•

Mourning spreads over burial grounds, incinerated mounds,
bleached indigenous bones scattered under dessicated pine
needles, trained dogs nosing into the past.
Touching adjacent fields, I sleep on haunted embankments.

•

Flames burning,
torch blooming, candelabra of the skyline—
I shine a flashlight into the back of the cupboard,
scumble through dust for a lost box of Cheerios.
Forgotten milk waits like forgiveness in the refrigerator.
Where is comfort—aroma of baking koláce and strudl,
caraway seed in sauerkraut, wild mushrooms in kuba,
warm round loaves of rye bread?

·

Crusted folds of skin over skin,
spreading fingers, thumb, sheathed in leather,
tan creases, lifelines cross the palm of the land—
names loom from tattered nights and overlapping
waves of oceans—bright immutable womb.

Fredrick Zydek

A Few Words For My Mortician

I prefer not to be drained like a beast
in the yards, but you may paint a flush
on my puckered skin, prop me on pillows
and keep the lights burning pink and low.

Tell them what a challenge my face became,
how you puffed up my cheeks with paraffin
and cotton, kept my lips and lids moist and
full with quick injections of a silicone

manufactured exclusively for your good house
of death. Tell them you didn't have to work
on my smile at all. Explain how the thing
took shape even as the last air quit moving.

Please play soft music. Debussy will do.
Place a ring of fresh daisies in my hair.
Insist I'm but in slumber, that it was my
custom to greet guests even in my dreams.

Father Dancing

My father liked to dance alone.
Late at night, when he was sure
the rest of the house was sleeping,
he would turn on the old Philco
and dance with the broom.

One summer, when mother sent me
out with his lunch, I caught him
doing the rumba in the berry patch.
Music seemed to come from his pores.
One winter, he waltzed for the cows.

I went to the barn to feed the cats.
I found him doing a perfect pirouette.
His arms spun out and up
until he was like a giant top
Spinning before the stalls.

168

The cows were lowing into their cuds.
I could tell they'd seen it all before.
Occasionally he would spin to a stop,
bow, kiss one of them right on the nose,
and two-step back into his turning.

One day I caught him dancing nude
in the small meadow down past our creek.
He and the dance were exquisite as prayer.
I thought of Noah's sons covering
their father's nakedness, and wondered why.

Mother at the Piano

She didn't play often
and she didn't play well.
Her right hand could read
everything in treble clef

except chords, rest signs,
quarter notes and tempo.
Her left hand was used
like a drum beating out

a waltz where a rumba
or fox-trot should be.
But she could pound out
a tune or two. If no one

was looking, melody
would flood the house
like relatives on a Sunday
afternoon. I would hide

in my room to listen.
She always sang off-key.
It didn't matter. When
Mother made music we

knew two things. She
was glad about something,
and for a little while
nothing needed dusting.

Biographies of the Poets

Lucy Adkins

Lucy Adkins grew up in rural Nebraska, attended country schools, the University of Nebraska, and received her degree from Auburn University in Alabama. Her poetry has been published in journals which include the *Owen Wister Review, Nebraska Territory, Northeast, South Dakota Review,* and the anthologies *Woven on the Wind, Times of Sorrow/Times of Grace, Crazy Woman Creek,* and the Poets Against the War anthology. Her chapbook, *One Life Shining: Addie Finch, Farmwife* is from Pudding House Publications. She lives in Lincoln where she works at an insurance company and devotes much of her time to writing poetry and fiction and tending her garden.

Susan Aizenberg

Winner of the 2003 Distinguished Artist Award from the Nebraska Arts Council, Susan Aizenberg is the author most recently of *Muse* (Southern Illinois UP), for which she was awarded the Nebraska Book Award for Poetry and the VCU Larry Levis Prize for 2003. Her first collection, *Peru,* appeared in Graywolf's *Take Three: AGNI New Poets Series,* and was chosen as a "Recommended Book" by both the Poetry and Small Press editors of Amazon.com, and as a "Noted Book" by *American Poet.* With Erin Belieu she is the editor of *The Extraordinary Tide: New Poetry by American Women* (Columbia University Press, 2001).

Denise Banker

Denise Banker took her PhD from the University of Nebraska—Lincoln in 2005. Her poems have appeared in *Prairie Schooner, Potato Eyes Literary Arts Journal* (now defunct), and some anthologies. She lives in Seward.

Carole Barnes-Montgomery

My pioneer heritage, the strong women who make up a great deal of my family history and my own years in the country raking hay, birthing calves and tending horses prepared me to write of the hardships females faced settling this country. My writing is also enriched through my work with the Nebraska State Historical Society where I am an active docent. Sharing Nebraska history with fourth grade students is a challenging and fulfilling pastime in retirement. I belong to three writing groups and enjoy my voyages into publication and the camaraderie of my writer pals.

GRACE BAUER

Grace Bauer's recent books include *Retreats & Recognitions* (Lost Horse Press, 2007), which won the 2006 Idaho Poetry Prize Competition, and *Beholding Eye* (CustomWords, 2006). She is also co-editor (with Julie Kane) of the anthology *Umpteen Ways of Looking at a Possum: Critical and Creative Responses to Everette Maddox*. Her poems, stories and essays have appeared in numerous anthologies and journals. She teaches creative writing, literature, and women's studies at the University of Nebraska-Lincoln.

STEPHEN C. BEHRENDT

Stephen C. Behrendt is George Holmes Distinguished Professor of English at the University of Nebraska-Lincoln. A widely published scholar of the literature and arts of the British Romantic period, he is also the author of three collections of poetry, *Instruments of the Bones* (1992), *A Step in the Dark* (1996), and *History* (2005), all published by Mid-List Press, Minneapolis. His poetry has appeared in many literary journals.

BRIAN E. BENGTSON

Actor, playwright and poet, Brian E. Bengtson is a native of Omaha, and has been featured in many national, Gay/Lesbian, and HIV/AIDS journals, such as *Hurakan*, *David's Place, Bay Windows*, and *Poetry Motel*. The Crawlspace Theatre in New Orleans first produced his one-act play, entitled *FAGS IN THE MALL*, in 1991. He served four and a half years as Poetry Editor for *The New Voice of Nebraska* (the state's oldest and longest-running G/L/B/T magazine until it folded in 1998).His first chapbook, entitled *Gay...Some Assembly Required,* was published by Lone Willow Press in 1995. His new book of poetry is *First Chill* (Publish America).He now lives in Omaha with his partner Chris, and his dog Lucy, who now must share her home with two new cats because she lacks an opposable thumb.

SHIRLEY J. BUETTNER

Although she was born in Kansas, Shirley Buettner has been a Kearney, Nebraska, resident since 1945. She completed her B.A. in Education degree at Nebraska State Teachers College in 1956 and an M.A. at Kearney State College, now the University of Nebraska at Kearney (UNK), in 1984. She taught in the UNK English Department for eight years. Shirley learned how to write poetry under the direction of Nebraska poet Don Welch, has published in small presses and in several anthologies. Juniper Press, LaCrosse, Wisconsin, published her two books, *Walking Out the Dark,* and *Thorns*. Both feature poems about farm and family.

Ron Block

Ron Block grew up in Gothenburg, Nebraska, where his mother was a reading teacher and his father a farmer and builder of livestock working equipment. The author of *Dismal River: A Narrative Poem* and *The Dirty Shame Hotel and other Stories*, he has received fellowships from the Nebraska Arts Council and the National Endowment for the Arts. His poetry has appeared in *The Southern Review*, *The Iowa Review*, *Epoch*, *Prairie Schooner*, *North Dakota Quarterly*, and *Ploughshares*. After living in Kennebunkport, New Orleans, Syracuse, Minneapolis, Fargo, Milwaukee, and North Platte, he currently lives with his wife and two sons in Pitman, New Jersey, where he teaches writing at Rowan University.

John Brehm

Originally from Lincoln, and a graduate of UNL, John Brehm is the author of *Sea of Faith,* which won the 2004 Brittingham Prize from The University of Wisconsin Press, and of *The Way Water Moves*, a chapbook from Flume Press. His poems have appeared in *Poetry*, *The Gettysburg Review*, *The Southern Review*, *Boulevard*, *The Missouri Review*, *Prairie Schooner*, *The Best American Poetry 1999*, and many other journals. He is a freelance writer and the Associate Editor of *The Oxford Book of American Poetry*. He lives in Brooklyn, New York.

Robert Brooke

Robert Brooke is Professor of English at the University of Nebraska-Lincoln, where he directs the Nebraska Writing Project. He has published four books and over forty articles on the teaching of writing, including *Rural Voices: Place-Conscious Education and the Teaching of English (NY: Teachers College Press, 2003)*, a collection featuring community-classroom projects throughout Nebraska. In his work for the Nebraska Writing Project, he has sponsored numerous writing workshops for children, teachers, and community members across the state; published yearly informal anthologies of teachers' creative writing; and provided mini-grants to improve writing in the state's schools.

Amy Knox Brown

A fourth generation Nebraskan, Amy Knox Brown holds a Ph.D. in English/creative writing from the University of Nebraska and a J.D. from Nebraska's College of Law. Her fiction, nonfiction and poetry has appeared in *Missouri Review*, *Other Voices*, *Shenandoah*, and other literary magazines. Brown's collection of stories, *Three Versions of the Truth*, was published in fall of 2007 from Press 53. An assistant professor of creative writing and English at Salem College, she currently lives in Winston-Salem,

J. V. Brummels

J. V. Brummels' poems have been widely published in journals and magazines and have been recognized with a number of awards, including a Literature Fellowship from the National Endowment for the Arts and the Mildred Bennett Award for contributions to the state's literature from the Nebraska Center for the Book. A new collection, his fourth, *Book of Grass* is due out this year. Raised first on a farm and later on a ranch, he was educated at the University of Nebraska. After college, he went East to Syracuse University to pursue a graduate degree in creative writing. In 1984 he and his wife, Lin, fulfilled a lifelong dream and began a horseback cattle ranch, which they still operate.

A longtime professor at Wayne State College, he has also written and published short fiction and a novel. For the last twelve years he's been the publisher of Logan House, which specializes in contemporary American poetry and short fiction. In 2006 he was named editor of the newly created WSC Press.

Michael Catherwood

Michael Catherwood lives and works in Omaha. He has won 2 Lily Peter Fellowships from the University of Arkansas, the Intro Award for Poetry from AWP, the Holt Prize for Poetry, was a finalist for the Ruth Lilly Collegiate Prize, and in 2003 he received an Artist's Fellowship from the Nebraska Arts Council. He has published in *Agni, Black Warrior Review, Borderlands, Briar Cliff Review, Georgetown Review, Louisiana Literature, Main Street Rag, Midwest Poetry Review, Pennsylvania English, Red River Review, South Dakota Review, Sycamore Review, Westview,* and others. His book *Dare* was published by The Backwaters Press in 2006.

James Cihlar

James Cihlar holds a BA from the University of Iowa, where he studied in the Writers Workshop, and a PhD from the University of Nebraska. He has taught at the University of Wisconsin in Stevens Point, as well as at the University of Minnesota in Minneapolis. His poems have appeared in *Prairie Schooner, Quercus, Red Owl, Water-Stone Review, Bloom, Briar Cliff Review,* and in the anthologies *Aunties* (Ballantine 2004) and *Regrets Only* (Little Pear Press 2006). He has won awards from the Academy of American Poets and the Minnesota State Arts Board.

Marilyn Coffey

Coffey is the author of three books, four chapbooks, hundreds of articles, stories, and poems. Her work has been published in England, Australia, India, Japan, Canada, Denmark, and the U.S. Her best-known poems are "Pricksong," a Pushcart Press winner, and *The Cretan Cycle: Fragments Unearthed from Knossos,* a book-length poem (Bandanna Press, Santa Barbara CA, 1991). More than 140 of Coffey's poems have been published in anthologies, newspapers, and journals such as *New American Review, Sunbury, New England Journal,* and *Manhattan Poetry Review.* The Archives, University of Nebraska Libraries, Lincoln, holds her manuscripts in its Marilyn Coffey Collection.

Shelly Clark Geiser

Shelly Clark Geiser received an MA in journalism at UNL and BA from UNK. She taught high school for 15 years and during her tenure she was a recipient of the Peter Keiwit Teacher Achievement Award for Excellence in Classroom Teaching and two-time winner of a Cooper Foundation Excellence in Teaching Award. She was also an instructor at Midland Lutheran College in Fremont, Nebraska, before devoting full time to her business. She and Marjorie Saiser are the co-editors of *Road Trip Conversations With Writers,* (The Backwaters Press, 2003), which received two Nebraska Center for the Book awards in 2004. Shelly's poems have appeared in *Nebraska Territory, Nebraska English Journal* and *Plains Song Review.* Her work has been anthologized in *Times of Sorrow/Times of Grace.* Shelly and husband, Jack, live in Omaha. She has two daughters, Haley and Elizabeth.

Elizabeth Clark Wessel

Elizabeth Clark Wessel was born in Imperial, Nebraska and has been living in Stockholm, Sweden for the past four years. She received a BA in creative writing from Sarah Lawrence College in 2002. She has worked as an editor at the art magazine *Livraison.* Her poems have appeared in the Sarah Lawrence Review and in the collection *Times of Sorrow/Times of Grace.* Clark Wessel is the editor of Stray Dog Press, an English language press based in Stockholm, Sweden. The first book from the press, in early 2008, will be *A Sky That is Never the Same,* prose poems by S.C. Hahn.

Paul Dickey

Paul Dickey's poems have appeared in about fifty online and print journals, including recent publications in *Sentence, Cue, Southern Poetry Review, Rattle, and The Cider Press Review.* Although he published in the 1970s in the quality journals of the region—*Kansas Quarterly, Quartet, and Nimrod, his* first chapbook *What Wisconsin Took* was released in June, 2006, by *The Parallel Press* of the University of Wisconsin-Madison Libraries. Two other collections *They Say This is How Death Came Into the World* and *Images of Knowing* have been named finalists in recent national chapbook competitions. Dickey has lived in Omaha since 1985, is married, and has three adult children.

Marilyn Dorf

Marilyn Dorf grew up on the farm her great grandparents homesteaded near Albion, Nebraska. Her writing has appeared in various publications, including *Kansas Quarterly, Willow Review, Plainsongs, Whole Notes, Northeast, South Dakota Review, Potpourri, 100 Words, Angel Face, Bison Poems, Plains Song Review, Nebraska Life, The Christian Science Monitor,* and the anthologies *Times of Sorrow/Times of Grace* and *Crazy Woman Creek.* She is the author of four chapbooks: *A Tribute to Buttons — A Beautiful Friend* (1985), *Windmills Walk the Night* (1992), *Of Hoopoes and Humming-birds* (1998), and *This Red Hill* (Juniper Press, 2003). She lives in Lincoln, Nebraska.

Lorraine Duggin

Lorraine Duggin lives in Omaha. She's published poetry, fiction, memoirs, and non-fiction in *Prairie Schooner, North American Review, North Atlantic Review, Short Story International,* among others, and has been recipient of a Vreeland Award, Academy of American Poets First Prize, Mari Sandoz Prairie Schooner First Prize for short story, Pushcart Prize nomination, Maude Hammond Fling Fellowship, Nebraska Arts Council's Individual Artist Award, and other recognition. She holds a Ph.D. in English/Creative Writing from UN-L, is a Master Artist in Literature in Artists in Schools/Communities programs of the Nebraska and Iowa Arts Councils, and teaches ESL at Metropolitan Community College, South Omaha Campus.

Pat Hemphill Emile

Pat Hemphill Emile is Assistant Editor of *American Life in Poetry.* She also serves as an Editorial Assistant for *Prairie Schooner.* Her poems have appeared in *Hedge Apple* and *Times of Sorrow, Times of Grace: Writing by Women of the Great Plains/High Plains.*

Kelly Madigan Erlandson

Kelly Madigan Erlandson's poems and essays have appeared in *Prairie Schooner, Crazyhorse, Smartish Pace, CALYX, 32 Poems* and *Flyway.* She has been a writer in residence at Jentel Artist Residency Program, and KHN Center for the Arts. She was awarded a Nebraska Arts Council Fellowship in nonfiction in 2006. Kelly is the author of *Getting Sober: A Practical Guide to Making it Through the First 30 Days* (McGraw-Hill, 2007). For more information, visit www.KellyMadiganErlandson.com.

Becky Faber

An Iowan by birth, Becky has lived in Nebraska since 1971, both in the southeast part of the state and the west central section. She considers Lincoln to be "home." Her poems have appeared in *Small Brushes, So to Speak: a feminist journal of language and art, The Blue Collar Review, The Plains Song Review, Plainsongs,* the *Nebraska English Counselor,* and the anthologies *Nebraska Voices* and *Lyrical Iowa.* For over a decade she has been a manuscript reader for *Plainsongs* (published by Hastings College). A former secondary and university English teacher, Becky is an Assistant Director in Career Services at UNL.

Charles Fort

Charles Fort held The Distinguished Paul W. Reynolds and Clarice Kingston Reynolds Endowed Chair in Poetry at the University of Nebraska at Kearney from 1997 to 2007. He remains a tenured Professor of English at UNK. Fort's poetry has appeared in *The Best American Poetry 2000* and *The Best American Poetry 2003.* His awards include the Randall Jarrell Poetry Prize, The Open Voice Poetry Award, and the Mary Carolyn Davies Memorial Award from the Poetry Society of America. Fort's early years: the son of Clara Hutchinson Fort and Charles Fort, Sr. (a factory worker and barber) Fort was born and raised in New Britain, Connecticut. His childhood journey began in a working-class African-American home—he was a newspaper boy with 125 customers a day. His first job was as a photographer for the hometown daily, *The New Britain Herald,* where he published photographs before poems. He has also worked at Ace Cleaning Company, and has been a coin collector, snow shoveler, shoeshine boy, barber shop sweeper, gas pumper, maintenance factory worker, and a library assistant. He was a letter award winner in three sports: cross country, indoor track, and outdoor track at New Britain Senior High School for the Golden Hurricanes. Fort roamed the downtown, factory lots, neighborhoods, and railyards of New Britain reciting poems and was, at times, called a "Jock-Poet."

Gaynell Gavin

Gaynell Gavin's prose and poetry have appeared or are forthcoming in various publications such as *Prairie Schooner, North Dakota Quarterly, Fourth Genre, The Chronicle of Higher Education, Best New Poets 2006* (Charlotte: Samovar Press, 2006) and *Times of Sorrow, Times of Grace* (Omaha: The Backwaters Press, 2002). Gay's poetry collection, *Intersections,* was published in the 2005 Main Street Rag Editor's Choice Chapbook Series. Her memoir, *What I Did Not Say: Reflections of an Attorney-at-Large,* was a finalist for the 2003 Associated Writing Programs Award Series in Creative Nonfiction. She lives in Lincoln, Nebraska.

S.C. Hahn

S.C. Hahn is a native of a Nemaha County farm near the ghost town of St. Frederick. He lives in Stockholm, Sweden, where he works as a market analyst at a software company. His poems, prose poems and other works have appeared in anthologies and journals in the U.S. and Great Britain. His current projects include a collection of prose poems forthcoming from Stray Dog Press, as well as translations of Swedish prose poems by Tomas Tranströmer, Brigitta Trotzig, Carl-Erik af Geijerstam and others.

Twyla Hansen

Twyla Hansen's latest book is a poem-drawing collaboration with Paul Johnsgard, *Prairie Suite: A Celebration* (www.springcreekprairie.org). She has four previous books, including *Potato Soup* (The Backwaters Press, 2003), winner of the 2004 Nebraska Book Award for poetry. Her poems have appeared in numerous periodicals and anthologies, including *Prairie Schooner, Organization & Environment, Crazy Woman Creek* (2004, Houghton Mifflin), and *Poets Against the War* (2003, Nation Books. Her M.Ag. and B.S. degrees are from the University of Nebraska-Lincoln. Twyla lives in Lincoln where her wooded acre is maintained as an urban wildlife habitat, recognized by the 1994 Mayor's Landscape Conservation Award.

Neil Harrison

Neil Harrison's poems have appeared in a number of journals and anthologies and have been collected in *Story* (Logan House Press, 1995 &1996), *In a River of Wind* (Bridge Burner's, 2000), and *Into the River Canyon at Dusk* (Lone Willow, 2005). He writes both poetry and fiction, and teaches English and Creative Writing at Northeast Community College in Norfolk, Nebraska.

Art Homer

Raised in the Missouri Ozarks and the Pacific Northwest, Art Homer worked on trail crews, and as an ironworker before attending Portland State University and the University of Montana. Since 1982, he has taught poetry and nonfiction writing at the University of Nebraska at Omaha Writer's Workshop, where he was named a Regents Professor in 1995. WordTech Press published his fourth poetry book, *Sight is No Carpenter*, in November 2005. His nonfiction book, *The Drownt Boy: An Ozark Tale* (University of Missouri Press, 1994) was a finalist for the AWP Award in Creative Nonfiction. He and his wife, poet & fine press printer, Alison Wilson, grow grapes in a corner of their 80 acres. They have built their own house in the opposite corner. Art is the proud owner of an old pickup and a young chocolate Lab to ride in the back.

Don Jones

Don Jones was born in Kimball, Nebraska, in 1938. He taught English at the U of Nebraska-Lincoln where he won the Academy of American Poets Prize and the Vreeland Award. He then taught at Hastings, Carleton, and St. Olaf. He's also been a medical caseworker, postal clerk/carrier, and poet-in-residence. He's now retired in Pueblo, Colorado. He's had poems in *Prairie Schooner, Massachusetts Review, Southern Poetry Review, The Nation,* etc. His books *Medical Aid* and *Other Poems* (U of Nebraska Press) and *Miss Liberty, Meet Crazy Horse!* (Swallow/Ohio U Press) can be had @ bookfinder.com.

William Kloefkorn

William Kloefkorn is an Emeritus Professor of English at Nebraska Wesleyan University in Lincoln. He has published several collections of poetry, three memoirs, two collections of short fiction, and a book of children's Christmas stories. In the 1970's he initiated the Poets-in-the-Schools program in Nebraska, and he has read his work and conducted workshops in many colleges and universities across the country. Among his awards are three honorary doctorates. In 1982 he was named Nebraska State Poet by the Unicameral. He and his wife, Eloise, have two daughters and two sons and a wide assortment of well-behaved grandchildren.

Bruce Koborg

Bruce Koborg served in the Marine Corps quite some time ago and he has been involved in the Omaha poetry scene for approximately six years. *Army of One* was written during the summer of 2003, at a place called Phyliss' Musical Inn in Chicago. Bruce has worked in a series of cubicles for the past few years, and he writes when he can. Some of his work has been anthologized and some of it ends up only on bar napkins.

Ted Kooser

Ted Kooser was born in Iowa, but has lived in Nebraska for over forty years. He has published eleven books of poetry and three of nonfiction, as well as a number of limited editions. In 2004 he was named Poet Laureate Consultant in Poetry to the Library of Congress, and served two terms. In 2005 he was awarded the Pulitzer Prize in Poetry for *Delights & Shadows.* He currently is Presidential Professor of English at the University of Nebraska-Lincoln.

Greg Kosmicki

A native of Alliance, Greg Kosmicki's poems have been published in literary magazines, both print and on-line, since the 1970s. He is the author of six chapbooks and two books of poetry. He was awarded an Artist's Fellowship for his poetry from the Nebraska Arts Council in 2001 and 2006. His poems have been nominated for the Pushcart Prize, and Garrison Keillor has read his poems on "Writers' Almanac." Greg is the editor and publisher of The Backwaters Press. He and his wife Debbie live in Omaha, Nebraska, where they are both employed in the social work field. They are parents of three mostly grown children.

Greg Kuzma

Greg Kuzma has taught the writing of poetry to undergraduates at UNL since 1969. He continues to love his teaching. Beginning in 1994 he became Faculty Advisor to the Undergraduate Literary and Fine Arts Magazine *LAURUS*, and he will complete his tenure with issue 07/08, to be published in the summer of 2007. Greg began writing screenplays in 1995, and he has written 16, but sold none. He continues to work on "Bloomsberries," a film about Virginia Woolf and her to-the-death struggle against The Patriarchy, as well as a second film, concerned with the retreat of the French Army from Moscow in the winter of 1812.

Steve Langan

Steve Langan is author of *Freezing* (New Issues Press, 2001) and *Notes on Exile & Other Poems*, which received the Weldon Kees Award (The Backwaters Press, 2005). His poems have appeared in *Fence, Shade, Slope, Verse, Jacket, Columbia, Witness, Meridian, DoubleTake, CutBank* and *Diagram*. Langan serves as executive director of a Nebraska non-profit health agency, and he's on the teaching residency faculty of the University of Nebraska MFA in Writing program. Additionally, he's a doctoral student in the Health and Preventive Medicine section of the University of Nebraska Medical Center, where he's working on a long poem titled "The Medical Center."

James Magorian

James Magorian was born in Palisade, Nebraska. He attended the Universities of Nebraska, Illinois State, Harvard, and Oxford. He is the author of numerous poetry collections, including *The Hideout of the Sigmund Freud Gang* (Black Oak Press), children's books, and the satirical novel *Hearts of Gold* (Acme, 1996).

Mordecai Marcus

Mordecai Marcus, b. 1925 in Elizbeth, N.J., grew up mostly in Brooklyn. He holds degrees from Brooklyn College, New York, and Kansas Universities. He has taught at Rutgers, Kansas, Purdue, and Nebraska Universities and has lived in the Midwest since 1952. Married in 1955, he has a son and a daughter. He abandoned poetry writing in 1948 but resumed it in 1969, since when he has published some 600 poems in journals and anthologies and seven chapbooks. He has also published many articles and a book on Robert Frost's poems. He is retired from the University of Nebraska-Lincoln and has lived in Lincoln since 1965.

Clif Mason

Clif Mason lives with his wife, a painter and jewelry maker, in Bellevue, Nebraska. He is Professor of English and English Department Chair at Bellevue University, a private school near Omaha. He was a Fulbright Fellow to Rwanda, Africa, before the civil war and genocide. His poetry has appeared in many American and English magazines and in *From the Dead Before*, a Lone Willow Press chapbook. He has been fortunate to be awarded prizes from *Writers' Journal*, *SPSM&H*, *Plainsongs*, the Midwest Writers' Conference, and the Academy of American Poets. He also writes magical realist fiction.

Matt Mason

After earning his MA in Creative Writing from the University of California at Davis, Matt moved to Omaha where he lives with his wonderful wife Sarah and daughter Sophia. Over 100 magazines and anthologies have published his poems, including *Laurel Review, Prairie Schooner, The Morpo Review*, and the online edition of *Mississippi Review*. New Michigan Press released his chapbook *Mistranslating Neruda* in 2003 and Lone Willow Press put out *When The Bough Breaks* in 2005. His first full-length collection, *Things We Don't Know We Don't Know*, was released by The Backwaters Press in April, 2006.

Janelle M. Masters

A writer of creative nonfiction, short fiction, and poetry, with poems published in *Whole Notes, The Comstock Review, Theology Today, Potpourri, Prairie Schooner, Poetry Motel, Runes, Margie, Common Ground Review*, and elsewhere, Masters received a Merit Award for poetry from the Nebraska Arts Council in 2000, and one for prose in 2003. A native Nebraskan, she has also lived in California and Wyoming. Her degrees are from the University of Nebraska-Kearney and Claremont Graduate University. She lives in Hastings, Nebraska where she teaches at Hastings Senior High School.

David McCleery

David McCleery is the former host of "Voices of the Plains, Conversations with Nebraska Writers," on KZUM radio; and the Publisher/Editor of A Slow Tempo Press and of *Leaves of Grass*. A recipient of the Mayor's Art Award for Literature, he lives in Lincoln, where he is the Store Director of the world famous Russ's Market at 17th and Washington Streets.

Nancy McCleery

Nancy McCleery's six poetry collections include *Girl Talk*, The Backwaters Press, 2002; *Blown Roses,* bradypress, *2001; Polar Lights*, Transient Press, 1994 and *Staying The Winter,* Cummington Press, 1987. She has received Literary Fellowship Grants from Alaska and Nebraska Arts Councils (1980, 1986, & 1995) and her poetry has appeared in Musical Theatre Pieces and Visual Art. Nancy earned an MA in Creative Writing/ Poetry under poet Greg Kuzma at the University of Nebraska-Lincoln (1979). She has taught at the University level, in Community Arts Programs and now teaches privately in Lincoln. Nancy has a son, a daughter and two granddaughters.

R. F. McEwen

R. F. McEwen is currently in the Department of English and Humanities at Chadron State College, where he has taught for the past twenty years. He completed his graduate work in English at the University of Nebraska, Lincoln in 1986. Since then he has been a frequent contributor to *Prairie Schooner*. His poems have also appeared in *Kansas Quarterly, South Dakota Review, Melville Extracts*, and other journals. His book, *Heartwood and Other Poems* (A Slow Tempo Press, 1996) was featured on CBS's "Sunday Morning". He is currently at work producing a two-volume CD "The Stories and Songs of Joe Heaney," as well as working on a book-length manuscript *Bills Boys and Other Poems*. R. F. McEwen also continues to be active in his first trade, tree trimming, which he began in Chicago in 1962.

J. J. McKenna

McKenna is professor of English at the University of Nebraska at Omaha where he teaches contemporary literature, temperament theory, and creative nonfiction. His poetry has appeared in more than 30 literary and mainstream journals and magazines including *The Louisville Review, Hawaii Review,* and *Ideals Magazine.* His poem, "At the Japanese Gardens" was nominated for the 1999 Pushcart Prize.

John McKernan

John McKernan was born in and grew up in Omaha. He has taught at Marshall University in West Virginia since 1967. He has published his poems in dozens of periodicals including *The New Yorker, Paris Review,* and the *Atlantic Monthly.* He edits the poetry magazine *ABZ.* A volume of his selected poems, *Resurrection of the Dust,* has just been published by The Backwaters Press.

Sarah McKinstry-Brown

Sarah Mckinstry-Brown studied poetry at the University of New Mexico and the University of Sheffield, England. After receiving her BA in Creative Writing, she embarked on a tour performing in coffeehouses, colleges, bars, libraries, and bookstores across the country. In 2004, she won the Blue Light Poetry Prize for her collection, *When You Are Born.* McKinstry-Brown has had poems published everywhere from Albuquerque's city buses and Omaha bus benches, to literary journals and standardized tests. When she's not reading or teaching workshops across the Midwest, Sarah makes her home in Omaha, with her husband, Matt Mason, and their daughter, Sophia.

Sally Molini

Sally Molini began writing when she moved to Nebraska from California in 1994. She earned a BFA from the University of Nebraska Omaha's Writers Workshop, and an MFA from Warren Wilson College. Her poems have appeared or are forthcoming in *32 Poems, Southern Poetry Review, Calyx, Best New Poets, Many Mountains Moving, Salt Hill,* and elsewhere. Online journals include *Mad Hatters' Review, Boxcar Poetry Review, Tattoo Highway, DMQ Review,* among others. She lives in Omaha with her husband and their two sons and a retriever named Max.

Charlene Neely

Charlene Neely writes in her car, a favorite chair, on a napkin, a deposit slip (not much need for those anyhow), she writes with her right hand (which sometimes is her left hand), she writes in meetings, during church, on her lunch hour. Her poems have appeared in *Plains Song Review; Times of Sorrow/ Times of Grace; Dreams for our Daughters; Celebrate,* and many other publications.

Ernst Niemann

Has, among other things, taught at the University of Nebraska at Omaha and Dana College.

Terrance Oberst

Terrance Oberst received his M.A. in Creative Writing from the University of Nebraska at Lincoln in 1993. He currently facilitates a writing workshop at the F Street Recreational Center twice a month. He has published three volumes of poetry. The first, a chapbook, *Returning,* by mulberry press in 1994, a full collection, *Transcendencies,* by Pygmy Forest Press in 2000 and, finally, another full collection, *Kinship Patterns,* by AuthorHouse in 2005. He has always thought of his poetry as a kind of "Ariadne's thread through the dark labyrinth of the self."

Jan Pettit

Jan Pettit was raised in Wymore, a tiny dot on the map in the lower right-hand corner of Nebraska. She now lives and writes in Minneapolis, MN. Her poetry has appeared in *Great River Review, South Dakota Review, Rosebud Magazine, Tusculum Review* and online at *spinelessbooks.com.* She is a soon-to-be graduate of the MFA program at Hamline University and is married to jazz guitarist, Paul Renz. They have two young sons who love returning to their mother's wide-open, windy home state. Jan is currently working on a book of prose and photography titled *Nebraska: Excerpts from a Small Town.*

Amy Plettner

Amy Plettner graduated from the University of Nebraska-Lincoln with a Bachelor of Science in Human Development and Family Rehabilitation, and a Certification in

Gerontology from the University of Nebraska-Omaha. Amy was a closet writer for fourteen years until discovering Lincoln's rich and diverse writing community and coming to the belief that published bio's do not, by themselves, make writers.

Hilda Raz

Professor of English and Women's & Gender Studies at the University of Nebraska, Hilda Raz is Luschei Editor of *Prairie Schooner*. Her books include *What Becomes You*, (University of Nebraska) *Trans,* and *Divine Honors, (Wesleyan) What is Good,* (Thorntree) and the chapbook, *The Bone Dish* (State Street). Her latest book, *All Odd and Splendid* is just out from Wesleyan University Press.

Jim Reese

Jim Reese is an Assistant Professor of English, and Director of the Great Plains Writers' Tour, at Mount Marty College in Yankton, South Dakota, where he is Editor-in-Chief of *Paddlefish*. Reese's poetry and prose have appeared in numerous journals and anthologies including *New York Quarterly, Prairie Schooner, South Dakota Review,* and others. His most recent collection is *These Trespasses* (The Backwaters Press, 2005). Poems from this book were recently nominated for the Pushcart Prize.

Robert Ross

Bob Ross is a poet and fiction writer living in San Antonio. He is the author, with Margaret MacKichan, of *In The Kingdom of Grass*, a book of essays and photographs. He is currently revising a novel, working title *The Woman Who Knew Bob Hope*. It is set in the 1950s in a town a little bit like Ainsworth, Nebraska. He teaches at San Antonio College.

Marjorie Saiser

Marjorie Saiser's books are *Bones of a Very Fine Hand* (1999) and *Lost in Seward County* (2001), both from The Backwaters Press, and also a chapbook, *Moving On,* from Lone Willow Press. Saiser is co-editor of *Road Trip* and *Times of Sorrow/Times of Grace,* both from The Backwaters Press. Her poems have been published in *Prairie Schooner, Georgia Review, Smartish Pace,* and *Crab Orchard Review.* She has received the Nebraska Book Award, the Literary Heritage Award, and a merit award from the Arts Council. Four of her poems have been featured on Garrison Keillor's "Writers Almanac." Marjorie and her husband Don live in Lincoln.

Mark Sanders

Mark Sanders was born and raised in Nebraska. He has taught in high schools, colleges, and universities in Nebraska, Missouri, Oklahoma, Texas, and, currently, as a Professor of English at Lewis-Clark State College in Idaho. His most recent book of poems is *Here in the Big Empty* (The Backwaters Press, 2006). In addition to having numerous poems published in journals in the U.S., Canada, Great Britain, and Australia, Sanders has creative prose in such journals as *Glimmer Train, River Teeth,* and *Shenandoah.* He has been nominated for a Pushcart Prize three times.

Roy Scheele

Roy Scheele's poems in both verse and prose have appeared in such major journals as *Measure, Poetry, The Southern Review* and *Verse* and have been frequently anthologized. He has also published criticism as well as interviews with/profiles of such contemporary poets as Hayden Carruth, Miroslav Holub, and W.D.Snodgrass. He is Poet-in-Residence at Doane College in Crete.

Terry Lee Schifferns

I live south of the Platte River in the Big Bend Region of Nebraska and teach writing at Central Community College where my students amaze and inspire me. My poetry has been published in numerous literary journals including: *Many Mountains Moving, Black Bear Review, Poets On, Poetry Motel, and Kinesis* and anthologies: *Bison Poems, Jane's Stories, Times of Sorrow/Times of Grace,* and *Slamma Lamma Ding Dong.* The essay, "Is This Work?" appeared in *Leaning into the Wind: Women Write from the Heart of the West.* Today I'm still writing from the heart of the West.

Barbara Schmitz

Barbara Schmitz grew up in Plattsmouth and except for two years in Southern California has lived her whole life in the "Nebraska presence" and traveled to sacred, exotic places like Kashmir, India; Konya, Turkey; Bali, and Jerusalem with her Sufi guide. *How Much Our Dancing Has Improved* from The Backwaters Press won the 2005 Nebraska Center for the Book Poetry Award. Her other full-length poetry book, *How to Get Out of the Body,* was published by Sandhills Press in 1999. She taught at Northeast College in Norfolk for 30 years and coordinated the Visiting Writers Series there. She has had poems published in such journals as: *Prairie Schooner, Nebraska Review, River Styx, Kansas Quarterly,* and *Poetry Motel.*

Karen Gettert Shoemaker

Karen Gettert Shoemaker's fiction and poetry have been anthologized in *A Different Plain: Contemporary Nebraska Fiction Writers* and in *Times of Sorrow/Times of Grace*. Her short story collection *Night Sounds and Other Stories* was published in the United States by Dufour Editions in 2002 and in the United Kingdom by Parthian Books of Wales in 2006.

Michael Skau

Michael Skau is a Professor in the Department of English at the University of Nebraska at Omaha, where he has been teaching since 1973. He has published books of literary criticism on the Beat Generation poets Lawrence Ferlinghetti and Gregory Corso and articles on Ferlinghetti, Corso, Jack Kerouac, William Burroughs, Richard Brautigan, and Jerzy Kosinski. A chapbook of Skau's poems, *Me and God Poems*, was published by bradypress in 1990, and his poems have appeared in *Carolina Quarterly, Northwest Review, Paintbrush, Kansas Quarterly, Laurel Review, Sequoia, Texas Review, Blue Unicorn, and Passaic Review*, among many others.

James Solheim

James Solheim's books for children include *It's Disgusting—and We Ate It!* (Simon & Schuster) and *Santa's Secrets Revealed* (Carolrhoda). His writing for adults has won a Pushcart Prize and an Ingram Merrill Fellowship. His sixty publications include long poems in *The Kenyon Review* and *Northwest Review*, as well as works in *Poetry, The Missouri Review*, and *Poetry Northwest*. Besides writing, James Solheim performs Norwegian folk dance and writes four-part-harmony folk music. He has taught creative writing at Southern Illinois University and Washington University in Saint Louis. Born in North Dakota and raised in Maryville, Missouri, he now lives in Omaha. Web site: http://jamessolheim.com.

Judith Sornberger

Judith Sornberger's poetry collections are *Open Heart, Judith Beheading Holofernes, Bifocals Barbie: A Midlife Pantheon,* and *Bones of Light.* She edited *All My Grandmothers Could Sing/Poems by Nebraska Women* (Free Rein Press). Her poems have appeared in journals such as *Prairie Schooner, Puerto del Sol, Tiferet: A Journal of Spiritual, Feminist Studies, Literature,* and *Calyx: A Journal of Women's Literature.* She is Professor of English and Director of Women's Studies at Mansfield University of Pennsylvania.

Mary K. Stillwell

A Nebraska native, Mary K. Stillwell studied writing in both New York and on the Plains. Her publications include The Paris Review, Prairie Schooner, The Massachusetts Review, Confrontation, and The Little Magazine. Her collection of poems, Moving to Malibu, was published by Sandhills Press. She received her Ph.D. from the University of Nebraska-Lincoln, and has published various articles, interviews, and reviews, including "In-Between: The Landscape of Transformation in Ted Kooser's Weather Central," "Beyond the Absolute Good" (on Linda Hogan's poem, "Seeing Through the Sun"), "The Art of Alchemy: Transformation in the Poetry of Hilda Raz," "The Ecologies of Place in the Poetry of Kathleene West," and "When a Walk is a Poem: Winter Morning Walks, A Chronicle of Survival, by Ted Kooser." Her dissertation, "Being(s) in Place(s)," focuses on four contemporary Nebraska poets.

Terese Svoboda

Svoboda is the author of ten books of prose and poetry, most recently *Tin God*_(U. of Nebraska Press, 2006) and the *forthcoming Black Glasses Like Clark Kent.* Critic Geoffrey O'Brien named her first novel, *Cannibal,* one of the best books in print. Her honors include an O'Henry Prize for the short story, a nonfiction Pushcart Prize, a translation NEH grant, three NY Foundation for the Arts grants in poetry and fiction, a NYS Council for the Arts and a Jerome Foundation grant in video, the John Golden Award in playwriting, the Bobst Prize in fiction, the Iowa Prize in poetry, and the Graywolf Nonfiction Prize. Her translation of Nuer song, *Cleaned The Crocodile's Teeth,* was selected by Rosellen Brown for the NY Times' Writer's Choice column. She is a native of Ogallala, Nebraska.

Kim Tedrow

Kim Tedrow is a writer and mixed-media artist who moved to Nebraska in 2000 for a job relocation. Born and raised in Austin, Minnesota, she has also lived in Minneapolis and in the Washington DC area. Her daughter, Anna Rose, attends the University of Nebraska-Lincoln. She keeps a blog at kimtedrow.blogspot.com, and can be reached by email at kimtedrow@aol.com.

Ruth Thone

Born in Scottsbluff, NE., 1931, graduate Journalism School, University of Nebraska, author of three books, "Woman and Aging, Celebrating Ourselves," "FAT: A Fate Worse Than Death? Women, Weight, and Appearance", and essay collection "Being Home;" weekly columnist for Lincoln Star, 5 years; commentator on Nebraska Public Radio, 5 years; currently bi-monthly columnist for Lincoln JournalStar; community activist in social justice; Humanities speaker re Women and Aging; free-lance writer for Nebraska

Life, UNL Alumni Magazine, and various other publications. Married to attorney, former Congressman and Governor Charles, daughter Anna, Marie, and Amy, granddaughters Charlotte and Stella, sons-in-law Hans and Bohus.

JON VOLKMER

Originally from Nebraska City, he is the author of a poetry collection, *The Art of Country Grain Elevators* (Bottom Dog Press, 2006) and a travel memoir, *Eating Europe: A Meta-Nonfiction Love Story* (Parlor Press, 2006). His poems, short stories and essays have appeared in many journals, including *Parnassus, Carolina Quarterly, Texas Review* and *Prairie Schooner*. He has an MA in Creative Writing from Denver University, and a PhD in English from the University of Nebraska-Lincoln. He now lives in Pennsylvania, where he is Professor of English and Director of Creative Writing at Ursinus College, and the recipient of a 2007 Fellowship from the Pennsylvania Council on the Arts.

SARAH VOSS

An undauntable writer, Sarah has published poetry in various literary journals, including recent work (2006-07) in *The Mid-America Poetry Review, Thema, Earth's Daughters, Ellipsis,* and *The Neovictorian/Cochlea*. In 2005, Sarah received an encouraging, personal e-reject from *The New Yorker*. Considering it her big claim to poetic fame, she promptly framed and hung the letter on her office wall, where it radiates nonstop messages of inspiration. Sarah is also a semi-retired Unitarian Universalist minister and a recognized author and prize-winning teacher in the field of religion and mathematics/science. Her three published books, including *What Number Is God?* all contain a smidgen of her poetry.

LYNN OVERHOLT WAKE

Born in Omaha, Lynn Overholt Wake recently completed her Ph.D at UNL, writing on E. B. White's environmental imagination, with an essay on *Charlotte's Web* appearing in *Wild Things:Children's Culture and Ecocriticism* (2004). An ecocritical essay inspired by Sue Rosowki on "Neighbour Rosicky" is in *Teaching Cather*. Her poetry is included in *Times of Sorrow/Times of Grace*. She has a daughter, a son, a daughter-in-law and a son-in-law. She and her husband, J. P. Wehrman, live in Seward, where their dog, Walter, has long been widely recognized.

REX WALTON

Rex Walton has been writing poetry for nearly twenty years, beginning in the mid '80s as a student of UNL English professors Greg Kuzma, Marcia Southwick, Mordecai Marcus and Warren Fine. He co-edited the English Department's *LAURUS* undergraduate annual magazine with Season Harper. He has seen some poems in print, such as the *Plainsong*, the *Plains Song Review*, *the Colorado Review*, *Fine Lines*, and an online symposium, *the Middlewesterner*. A poem of his was used as the lyics for *Color of Silence*, a musical piece by Anthony Lanman. Walton also organized the Crescent Moon Reading Series for five years, a weekly gathering of poets, writers, and musicians.

COREEN WEES

Coreen Wees has had poems published in a number of literary journals, including the *South Dakota Review*, *The Midwest Quarterly*, *The Mid-America Poetry Review*, *The Platte Valley Review*, and *Pierian Springs*. She studied writing with Don Welch at Kearney State College, and with Art Homer at University of Nebraska at Omaha. She is also a former poetry editor for *The Nebraska Review.* She currently lives in Omaha with her husband, Greg, and their daughter Regina, and she teaches writing and literature at Iowa Western Community College.

DON WELCH

Don Welch was born in Nebraska and, after living in Texas, Maryland, Illinois, and Colorado, returned to his home state at an early age. The author of a number of books of poetry, his selected works appear in *Inklings* (Sandhills Press, 2001). Among his poetry prizes is the Neruda Prize for Poetry when judged by William Stafford. He was a poet-in-the-schools for 20 years, and he has taught English and Philosophy at the University of Nebraska at Kearney for almost 50 years.

KATHLEENE WEST

Kathleene West grew up on a farm three miles west of Genoa, Nebraska. As a Fulbright scholar, she lived in Iceland two years. She is Professor of English at New Mexico State University and Poetry Editor of *Puerto del Sol.* She has traveled extensively in, and translated poetry from Cuba, Mexico, and Central America. Current research has taken her to Russia and Ukraine. West has published ten books of poetry and prose; her novel, *The Summer of the Sub-Comandante,* was published in 2002, the year the family farm was sold.

JAN CHISM WRIGHT

Jan Chism Wright is a native of Houston, Texas who retired nine years ago, moved to a farm in southeast Nebraska and was seduced by the beauty of the land and the life she encountered. After a twenty-five year banking career, she is pursuing her dream of writing full-time and spending quality time with her husband and sixteen year-old daughter. Although she received a BBA in Economics from the University of Houston, she also took courses in creative writing there and at Rice University, St. Thomas University and, most recently, Peru State College. Her work has been published in the *Plains Song Review* put out annually by the University of Nebraska Press, *Your Country Neighbor* and the *Falls City Journal.*

David Wyatt

Born and grew up in Southern California, wanting to be a professional baseball player. Played one year of college ball at San Diego State, before flunking out. Three years in US Army, in Oklahoma and Vietnam. Oklahoma was hotter. Received BFA in creative writing from UNO. Held one-year teaching fellowship in poetry at University of Oregon. Poems published in *Cutbank, Carolina Quarterly, Alaska Quarterly Review, Prairie Schooner, Northwest Review, Poetry* and *Poetry East.* Received Distinguished Merit Award in Poetry from Nebraska Arts Council, 2006. A chapbook, *Approaching a Diner in Potsdam,* is coming out from Crying Dime Press. Wyatt works in the Criss Library at the University of Nebraska, Omaha.

Rosemary Zumpfe

Rosemary Zumpfe is a poet and artist living in Lincoln, Nebraska. She teaches creative writing at a local center for homeless women. Her hand-made poetry book, ThumB, was in the 2005 International Traveling Miniature Book Exhibition, and her work has appeared in *Times of Sorrow/Times of Grace* anthology and various literary magazines. She has just completed a book which combines poetry and mixed-media art, and she is in the process of writing her third collection of poetry.

Fredrick Zydek

Fredrick Zydek is the author of eight collections of poetry. *T'Kopechuck: the Buckley Poems* is forthcoming from Winthrop Press later this year. Formerly a member of the faculty in creative writing at UNO and later Lecturer in Theology at the College of Saint Mary, he is now a gentleman farmer when he isn't writing. He is the editor for Lone Willow Press.

Acknowledgements

Lucy Adkins
"On the Pleasant Valley Road": *Poet Lore*, Vol. 101, No. 3/4, 2006.

Susan Aizenberg
"Debut: Late Lines for a Thirtieth Birthday": *Muse* (Crab Orchard Poetry Series), Southern Illinois University Press, 2002.
"Things That Cannot Be Compared (Dissonance I) ": *Blackbird: An Online Journal of Literature and the Arts*, Virginia Commonwealth University, Vol. 3, No. 2, 2004.

Carole Barnes-Montgomery
"Any Particular Joy": *Poetry Pages*, Lincoln Chaparral Poets, Vol. 34, No. 10, 2006.

Grace Bauer
"On Finding a Footnote to Truckin'": *Arts & Letters*, Issue 7, 2002.
"Modern Clothing": *Puerto del Sol*, Vol. 40, No. 2, 2005.
Both poems reprinted in *Retreats & Recognitions*, Lost Horse Press, 2007.

Stephen C. Behrendt
"Hawk Shadow, Early May": *Puerto del Sol* Vol. 40, No. 1, 2005.
"The November Hawk": Reprinted by permission from *The Hudson Review*, Vol. 55, No. 4, (Winter, 2003). Copyright © by Stephen C. Behrendt.

Brian E. Bengtson
"A Cigarette with Loni": *First Chill*, PublishAmerica, 2005.

Ron Block
"Strip Joint": *Ploughshares*, Vol. 21, No. 1, 1995.
"Shame": *North Dakota Quarterly*, Vol. 62, No. 1, 1994-95.

John Brehm
"Sea of Faith": *The Southern Review*, Vol. 34, No. 2, 1998.
"Valid Photo Identification Required": *The Gettysburg Review*, Vol. 19, No. 2, 2006.
"Sea of Faith": *The Best American Poetry 1999*, Scribner's. Included in John Brehm's book of the same title, University of Wisconsin Press, 2004.

Amy Knox Brown
"Old Wives' Tales": *The Spoon River Poetry Review*, Vol. XXXI, No. 2, 2006.

J.V. Brummels
"Dakota, 1933": *South Dakota Review*, Vol. XLIV, No. 3, 2006.

Shirley Buettner
"Neighbor": *The Sandhills & Other Geographies, An Anthology of Nebraska Poetry*,
    Sandhills Press, 1978.
"October": *The Scrivener*, Vol. II, No. I, 1981-82.
Both poems reprinted in *Walking Out The Dark*, Juniper Press, 1984.

Michael Catherwood
"The Cement Evangelical Worship Center":
The Monday Poetry Report, http://www.mondaypoetryreport.com, Winter, 2003.

James Cihlar
"The Estate Auction": *The James White Review*, 1997.

Marilyn Coffey
"Pricksong": *Aphra*, Vol. 6, No. 2, 1975; reprinted in *The Pushcart Prize: Best of
    the Small Presses*, 1st Ed., 1976-77, Pushcart Press; *Potpourri*, Omega
    Cottonwood Press, 1989, 1990; *Parnassus of World Poets 1994*.

Paul Dickey
"Constellation": *Redactions*, Issue 4/5, 2005.

Marilyn Dorf
"Dawn Watch": *Whole Notes*, Vol. 15, No. 1, 1999.

Lorraine Duggin
"Steamer Trunk": Kosmas: Czechoslovak and Central European Journal, Vol. 12, No.
    2, 1997.

Kelly Madigan Erlandson
"Nebraska": *The Massachusetts Review*, Vol. XLV, No. 4, 2004-05.
"Twenty-Five Years Later, She Learns Her Ex is Dying," *Natural Bridge*, No. 15, 2006.

Becky Faber
"My Sister": *So to Speak: A Feminist Journal of Language and Art*, Vol. 15, No. 1,
    2006.

Charles Fort
"The Vagrant Hours" printed in *Center for Writers and Mississippi Review Poetry
Awards, 2002*, and reprinted in *The Best American Poetry 2003*, Charles Scribner's
and Sons.

Tom Gannon

A previous version of "Bird Poem" appeared in *The South Dakota Review*, 21.3, 1983, p. 87, and was reprinted in special issue of *The South Dakota Review: Poetry 1963-1991*, 29.3.ii, 1991, p. 68.

Gaynell Gavin

"Identification" : *The Comstock Review*, Vol. 15, #1, 2007.
"Military Secrets": *Words and Pictures*, Vol. 5, 2001.
    Both poems printed in *Intersections*, Main Street Rag, 2005.

Twyla Hansen

"Late Winter: Survival": *Midwest Quarterly*, Vol. 42, No. 2, 2001.
"Potato Soup": Reprinted from the *Prairie Schooner*, volume 73, Number 1, (spring 1999) by permission of the University of Nebraska Press. Copyright 1999 ©by the University of Nebraska Press.
"We Are On Nine-Mile Prairie When": *Plains Song Review*, Vol. 4, 2002; Film-illustrated for Nebraska ETV's *Next Exit*, 9/11/2002.
    All three poems reprinted in *Potato Soup*, The Backwaters Press, 2003.

Neil Harrison

"Naming the Lakes": *South Dakota Magazine*, May/June, 2005, reprinted in *Into the River Canyon at Dusk*, Lone Willow Press, 2005.

Don Jones

"Thousands at His Bidding Post": *Don Jones, 9 Postal Poems*, three sheets, a chapbook series, Lincoln, NE, No. 2, 1971.

William Kloefkorn

"Connections: A Toast": *Great River Review*, Fall/Winter, 1999-2000; reprinted in *Fielding Imaginary Grounders*, Spoon River Poetry Press, 2004.
"My Love for All Things Warm and Breathing": *The Spirit That Moves Us*, Vol. 5, 1979, reprinted in *Cottonwood County*, Windflower Press, 1979; *Treehouse: New and Selected Poems*, White Pine Press, 1996; *Walking the Campus*, Lone Willow Press, 2004.

Ted Kooser

"At the Cancer Clinic": *Delights and Shadows*, Copper Canyon Press, 2004.
"Etude": *Weather Central*, University of Pittsburgh Press, 1994.
"Selecting a Reader" and "So This is Nebraska": *Flying at Night*, University of Pittsburgh Press, 2005.

Greg Kosmicki

"Windows": *Nimrod*, Vol 47, no. 2, Spring/Summer 2004; reprinted in *Some Hero of the Past*, Word Press, 2006.

GREG KUZMA

"Let There Be an End to Excuses": *Skywriting.*
"Sometimes": *Shenandoah.*
Both poems reprinted in *A Horse of a Different Color,* Illuminati, 1983.
"When We Dead Awaken": *Poetry Northwest;* reprinted in *Wind Rain and Stars and the Grass Growing,* Orchises, 1993.

STEVE LANGAN

"Meet Me at the Happy Bar": *The Nebraska Review,* Spring, 2005.
"Notes on Landscape": *Fence,* Vol. 7, No.1, 2004.
"Notes on Lanscape" reprinted in *Notes On Exile and Other Poems,* Winner of The Weldon Kees Award, The Backwaters Press, 2005.

JAMES MAGORIAN

"Crickets": *Green Fuse* #24, March 1997.
"The Theory of Evolution": *Birmingham Poetry Review,* No. 12, 1994.

MORDECAI MARCUS

"Always Back There," *Poet Lore,* Vol. 83, No. 4, 1988.
"Seekers," *Journal of Evolutionary Psychology,* Vol. 1, 1984.

CLIF MASON

"Big Muddy": *The Briar Cliff Review,* Spring, 2000.
"The Old Crow": *Riverrun,* Summer, 1999.

MATT MASON

"The Good News": *Poet Lore,* Summer, 2003. Reprinted in *Things We Don't Know We Don't Know,* The Backwaters Press, 2006.

JANELLE MASTERS

"The Body": Reprinted from the *Prairie Schooner,* volume 73, number 1 (Spring 1999) by permission of the University of Nebraska Press. Copyright 1999 © by the University of Nebraska Press.

R. F. McEWEN

"John Davis": Reprinted from the *Prairie Schooner,* volume 73, number 1 (Spring1999) by permission of the University of Nebraska Press. Copyright 1999 © by the University of Nebraska Press.
"John Early Remembers the Moment of His Wife's Death": *Prairie Schooner,* Vol. 80, No. 1, 2006.

John McKernan

"Walking Along the Missouri River North of Omaha I Find an Indian Arrowhead":
    Antaeus, Vol. 17, 1975.
"I Would Trade Places With Your Death.": *The Georgia Review,* Fall, 2001.
"I Chose the Gyroscope Because It Was Holy": Reprinted by permission from
    The Hudson Review, Vol. 58, No. 3, (Autumn, 2005). Copyright © 2005 by
    John McKernan.

Sarah McKinstry-Brown

"Music Appreciation 101": KE5TRA [Sound Literature], December, 2005.

Sally Molini

"Silk Shop on the Ganges": *Tar River Poetry,* Vol. 2, No. 44; reprinted in *Best New
    Poets Anthology, 2005,* Samovar Press, Charleston, Virginia, in cooperation
    with *Meridian.*

Nancy McCleery

"Girl Talk (aristotle)": letterpress broadside, bradypress, 1994.
"Girl Talk (lists)": *Girl Talk,* The Backwaters Press, 2002.
"Girl Talk (nine/9)": *Blown Roses,* bradypress, 2001. All three poems reprinted in
    Girl Talk, The Backwaters Press, 2002.

Charlene Neely

"Unraveling": *Celebrate: A Collection of Women's Writings,* Vol. VII, University of
    Nebraska, Omaha, Program for Women and Successful Aging.

Terrance Oberst

"Death and Company," *Plainsongs,* Vol. 12, #2, p. 21

Jan Pettit

"Listening to the voices of poets long dead": *South Dakota Review,* Vol. 44, 2006.

Hilda Raz

"For Barbara, Who Brings a Green Stone in the Shape of a Triangle": *Divine
    Honors,* Wesleyan University Press, 1998.
"Pets," *All Odd and Splendid,* Wesleyan University Press, 2008.

Jim Reese

"Strike on the Stoop": *Plains Song Review,* Vol. IV, 2002.
"Ten Penny High": *New York Quarterly,* No. 61, 2005.
    Both poems reprinted in *These Trespasses,* The Backwaters Press, 2005.

Marjorie Saiser
"Paradise on the Niobrara" and "My Father Argued with my Mother": *Prairie Schooner,* Vol. 81 Summer, 2007.
"Night Flight": *Lost in Seward County,* The Backwaters Press, 2001.

Mark Sanders
"Custody," "Death's Door," and "Talking November Weather, Long Distance": *Here in the Big Empty,* The Backwaters Press, 2006.

Roy Scheele
"At the North Edge of Town": *Tennessee Poetry Journal,* Vol. 3, No. 1, 1969.

Barbara Schmitz
"Supper": *How to Get Out of the Body,* Sandhills Press, 1999.
"How to Get to Plattsmouth": *How Much Our Dancing Has Improved*, The Backwaters Press, 2004.

Michael Skau
"Winter at Ram's Horn Mountain": *Paintbrush,* Vol. 15, No. 30, 1988.

James Solheim
"Blessed by Meteors and by the Benevolent Men of Space":
Poetry, Vol. 6, No. 156, 1990.

Judith Sornberger
"Our Lady of the Rest Stop": *White Pelican Review;* reprinted in *On the Road: Pre-owned Auto-related Poems*, Issue 8, Pelican Review.
"Wallpapering the Patsy Cline": *Calyx: A Journal of Art and Literature by Women,* Vol. 12, No. 3, 1990; reprinted in Open Heart, Calyx Books, 1993.

Mary K. Stillwell
"Circle Dance," *Literal Latté,* 1995; reprinted in *Crazy Woman Creek,* Gaydell Collier, Nancy Curtis, Linda Hasselstrom, Eds., Houghton-Mifflin, 2004; and in *Times of Sorrow/Times of Grace,* Greg Kosmicki, Marjorie Saiser, Lisa Sandlin,Eds., The Backwaters Press, 2002.
"The Red Barn," *Times of Sorrow/Times of Grace,* Greg Kosmicki, Marjorie Saiser, Lisa Sandlin, Eds., The Backwaters Press, 2002.

Kim Tedrow
"Recent Angels": Reprinted from *Prairie Schooner,* Volume 77, number 1, (spring 2003) by permission of the University of Nebraska Press. Copyright 2003 © by the University of Nebraska Press.

Jon Volkmer
"Cosmology" and "Fumigant": *The Art of Country Grain Elevators,* Bottom Dog Press, 2006.

Don Welch
"Funeral at Ansley": *Dead Horse Table,* Windflower Press, 1975.
"Nebraska": *The Rarer Game,* Kearney State College Press, 1980.
"The Keeper of Miniature Deer": *The Keeper of Miniature Deer,* Juniper Press, 1986.

Kathleene West
"Progression": *The Farmer's Daughter,* Sandhills Press, The Plains Poetry Series, Vol. 7. 1988.

David Wyatt
"Enough Driving": *Ninth Letter,* Vol. 2, No. 2, 2005.
"Man With Green Thumb": *Epicenter,* Vol. 9, 2005.

Fredrick Zydek
"Mother at the Piano": *The Antioch Review,* Vol. 63, No. 4, 2005.
"A Few Words for my Mortician": *Poetry,* 1997.
"Father Dancing": *Sojourners,* 1996.

CPSIA information can be obtained at www.ICGtesting.com
Printed in the USA
BVOW09s1950060616

450948BV00005B/16/P